Don't Let the Blue Star Turn Gold

Don't Let the Blue Star Turn Gold

Downed Airmen in Europe in WW II

Jerry W. Whiting

7/25/16

Edited by: Dr. Elliott S. Dushkin
Front cover art by: Peter Kassak
Photo restoration by: Laura Sharpe

Book Design by Falcon Books

San Ramon, California

ISBN 978-0-6926574-9-2

Second Edition

Library of Congress Control Number 2005930197

Published by
TARNABY
2576 Fox Circle
Walnut Creek, CA. 94596
EAJWWhiting@aol.com

PRINTED IN THE UNITED STATES OF AMERICA

To all the Fallen Stars and to
those who showed them kindness.

Table of Contents

Acknowledgements

This book simply couldn't have been written without the assistance of many friends and colleagues, both here and abroad. I am particularly proud of those of my generation who came to my assistance, providing photos, background information, resources, documents and research assistance so the following generations may know about the past. I have listed my overseas colleagues separately, so that the magnitude of the European assistance can be known. I believe it may also be of interest to know where these people are living today, so I have listed their country of residence.

C.D. Adams	Mike Adams
Freda Anagnost	Van Anagnost
Robert Anderson	Bob Bobier
Judy Birdsong	Daniel Blodgett
George Brandon	Jack Breen
John Bybee and SPG	Paul Canin
Vernon Christensen	Lynn Cotterman
Dan Crouchley	Bill Culver
Hank Dahlberg	Richard Doyle
Bill Forsythe	Mary Gordon
Bruce Hale	Randy Hannum
William Herblin	Ray Heskes
Robert Hickman	Bonnie Hollenbeck

Burl Jackson

Bob Johnson

Ben Karoly

Mike Knab Sr.

Mark LaScotte

William MacLean

Daniel Mortensen

Sherri Ortegren

Frank Pratt

John Reifer

William T. Ryan

Sammy Schneider

Steve Sharpe

Murray Sheridan

Tony Siller

Warren Sortomme

Yolanda Lubanovich Stahl

Robert Tharratt

Rebecca Uslan

Hal Ware

Ann Whiting

Zdzislaw Jarkiewicz

John Jones

Harold Kempffer

Gerald Landry

Marvin Lindsay

Sheree Matousek

Albert O'Brien

Charles Palmer

Art Rasco

Joseph Russell

James Scheib

Laura Sharpe

Charlene Shelor

Daniel Sjodin

Ray Slominski

Roland Stumpff

Tom Tabor

Leslie Uslan

Lisa Walker

Jack Whatley

Doug Whiting

AFRHA Maxwell AFB, Alabama (with a special thanks to Lynn Gamma and her staff)

485th Bomb Group Association

European assistance provided by:

Igor Bartosik, Poland
(MuseumAuschwitz-Birkenau)

D'Olivo family-Italy

Laura Fuerst-Austria

Ryszard Goralczyk, Poland

Hrvoje Hrelic-Croatia

Peter Kassak, Slovakia

Karlo Kotlar-Croatia

Marino Kvarantan, Croatia

Zygmunt Kraus, Poland

Roberto Lerga, Croatia

Sime Lisica, Croatia

Venci Lonic, Croatia

Jakob Mayer, Austria

Waldemar Ociepski, Poland

Ken Petersson, Sweden

Bolestaw Rudek, Poland

Alisja Serwatka, Poland

Szymon Serwatka, Poland

Stanimir Stanev, Bulgaria

Fabio Stergulc, Italy

Maria Stryzynska, Poland

Krzysztof Wielgus, Poland
(Krakow Air Museum)

Stefan Wiktor, Poland

Georg Hoffman, Austria

Special thanks are also in order for A.M.I.A.P. (Aircraft Missing in Action Project). This is a group of serious volunteers in Poland, who specialize in locating American aircraft that went down in Poland in WWII. They go far beyond their stated purpose, doing extensive research on the airmen who went down and providing information to interested American researchers. (http://www.samoloty.ow.pl/amiap/)

Prologue

The writer sat quietly in his chair, laptop in front of him, pondering his next sentence. It was late in the evening and he was alone. Being tired, the writer leaned back for a moment, lost in thought. Then it happened, something he would never comprehend.

He had been working on the stories for a long time. All were carefully researched and the writer worked diligently to recreate the stories, to be faithful to the truth. It had not been easy and it was a long, arduous process. His deadline neared and he had to complete his manuscript. When it happened, it seemed so real. It just couldn't be............

He found himself standing there, watching them. It seemed so natural. He was among them in a field, but he wasn't one of them. There were two groups of flyers in this grassy field, surrounded by hedges and trees. It was foggy and cold and smelled of morning. He slowly walked between the two groups of airmen, watching their actions. They were large groups and spread out. Both groups wore their flying clothing, but were not interacting. This didn't seem unusual to the writer, but neither did his presence there.

One group of airmen seemed more active. Some were talking about flying, using their hands to describe their maneuvers in the air. A few others were tossing a softball around. There was joking and laughter.

The men in the second group appeared tired. A few talked quietly. Many sat on their B-4 bags. A few stretched out on the grass, using their parachutes or heavy leather jackets as headrests. They didn't seem particularly sad, just tired and more serious than the first group. The writer walked through the second group, but no one seemed to notice him. Some looked vaguely familiar to the writer, but they couldn't be. They were from a past generation. A few looked similar to men he had seen in old photos, standing or kneeling in front of their bombers.

As the writer walked across the field to watch the more active group, he heard a loud voice booming out across the field. All activity ceased and both groups looked up when they heard the voice, demanding their attention.

The voice began calling out names. Individual flyers from the second group stood up as their names were called, grabbed their gear and began walking to a clearing at one corner of the field. The voice continued calling names. "Alfred Bertelli, Richard Boehme, Ormiston Brown, John Crouchley....," and the list went on. Some of the names sounded familiar to the writer as he watched the men slowly walk away.

Some of the men in the first group appeared confused. The writer stood at the edge of this group and watched men from the other group walk across the field. One of the airmen said "It's not fair. It just ain't right," and shook his head in disgust. "You're right," another retorted, "For us it's always hurry up and wait. Must be another snafu." The roll call continued, heard above the grumbling in the group. "Arthur Daehn, Donald Demmler, William Eggers, Earl Franquet, Lawrence Griggs....," The list seemed endless as the men walked single file across the grass.

The dissention continued. A young sergeant asked of no one in particular, "What's so special about them?" Another airman, wearing the wings of a bombardier, exclaimed "Wait a minute! He went down!" A pilot answered "You're right! I saw him! The fighters at Munich got him." Others began talking as they recognized names. The voice continued, louder now. "Matthew Hall, Richard Hardman, Edward Hope, Jack Hubbard, Richard Irmen, Merwin Jacobson, Lewis Kaplan, James Lazarakis, William Lawrence....," and the list went on.

The writer shuddered as he recalled why some of the names were familiar. Some were men he was writing about. They were all dead. All those walking away were dead! He watched and listened as more names were called and saw the men stand, grab their gear and walk off. He recognized a few faces from the photos. "Everett MacDonald, Eugene Maylath, James McNulty, Francis Meech, Harold Oliver, Donald Palmer, Rosario Spano....," and the voice continued. The voice was so loud now the writer's ears were hurting, "Donald Swenson, John Tomhave, Elvis Waisath, Robert Ware....," louder and louder. Then there was silence.

The entire second group had passed through the clearing. They were gone, every single one of them. A young captain walked away from the remaining group, toward the clearing. The writer followed at a distance, his ears still ringing. As the captain approached the clearing, the voice commanded, "Stop!" The captain stopped, temporarily losing his composure. The captain asked, "Why do they get to go? Why can't the rest of us go?" The voice slowly and clearly answered, "It's not your turn. You're not finished yet. You have to tell their stories."......

The writer sat up in his chair. The airmen were gone. It seemed so real. It couldn't be. He didn't believe in things like that and it didn't make sense, but with renewed vigor he started writing.......... and vowed to help them tell their stories.

INTRODUCTION

Why do we continue to tell the stories of these men and their widows and wives, focusing on that brief period of their lives known as WWII? To see the survivors, most don't look like the leading men and women in our movies today. Is it because they're our parents, grandparents, friends or relatives and we want to know more about them? Is it because the stories are of simpler times? Might it be that there are lessons we can learn? Is it because they experienced an important part of history? All the above were factors when I decided to write this book. This, coupled with the fact that some are still with us, led me to embark upon this journey.

I call it a journey because it took me to various places physically, emotionally, spiritually and intellectually. All were places I had not visited before. Some I will visit again. It's difficult to keep one's own beliefs out of a story when writing about others; in fact, it's nearly impossible. I have this "thing" about telling the truth and writing the truth. I know this is from my own background, yet it sometimes gets in the way of telling a good story. When I look at some of the best sellers today I see lots of quotes about what people were saying 60-plus years ago. You won't see much of that in this book. The survivors recall clearly their thoughts at the time, but few recalled the specific words that were said.

Fortunately, records do exist for many of the stories. Those who escaped or evaded capture routinely completed a statement upon their return. Returning airmen who witnessed an aircraft going down made written statements at debriefing. This information is extremely beneficial when one endeavors to tell a true story, because it is history recorded as (or shortly after) it occurred. Diaries kept at the time are of equal benefit. This information coupled with memories, should create a story that is accurate, yet interesting. You, the reader, must be the judge of that.

While writing my first book about airmen in the 15th Air Force, I interviewed many men who told me of watching bombers go down over Germany or other occupied countries. For many, it was a simple fact; the crew was gone. Whether friends, acquaintances or just comrades in arms, they were gone. They didn't dwell on it. I won't try to understand their feelings, but some expressed them in various ways, ranging from "those poor bastards", to "at least it's over for them", to "I was just glad it wasn't me". Sometimes it really was over for the crew that went down and all perished. In other cases there were survivors, even when no parachutes were seen spilling from the stricken aircraft. Regardless of whether they lived or died, the airmen who flew with them didn't know what happened to them until later, if at all.

It was during some of these early interviews that the men wondered aloud what happened to the crew of the plane that was last seen in a fatal, flaming dive or a flat spin, or lagging behind the formation with two engines smoking. It was as if they hadn't thought about them for many years. I also wondered what happened to them. That's the topic of this book.

What you will read are some of these stories. They're all from the same bomb group, the 485th, although some of the stories incorporate information from airmen from other bomber and fighter groups in Italy and England. These are just a few stories, taken from various squadrons, but representative of all those "fallen stars". A primary reason for choosing this group is that my dad, Wayne Whiting, was a tail gunner in the 485th Bomb Group. With his association to the group, finding the survivors and/or their families became much easier. From my earlier research I felt I had also developed some credibility and trust.

The word "honor" comes to mind. I am so honored to be able to present these stories in written form. This is truly my reward for this effort. My ego soars to think these fine airmen and/or their families trusted me to share their memories. Some of the stories have been told in written form, but most haven't, at least not in depth. Some veterans hadn't shared much about their experiences and were understandably reluctant to talk about these life-altering events so long ago, especially with a stranger and novice writer. I'm grateful they trusted me.

It can be painful to recall those emotions of seeing that telegram advising that a loved one was Missing in Action. It wasn't easy for a returning POW to tell the wife of a buddy, still waiting for an answer, that her husband definitely was killed and there was no hope he had survived.

Most of us have never known true hunger. We don't know what it's like to have no food at all for two or three days, or to be isolated in solitary confinement with no one on our side knowing we're alive. That's another kind of hunger. Imagine being seriously injured on a snowy hillside in a foreign land with no one near to help or, worse yet, being seriously injured in captivity and denied medical treatment. It would be difficult for any of us to imagine what it must feel like to be pursued by German soldiers after escaping from them, or what emotions would run through our minds if we were bombed or strafed by our own troops.

Yet, there were often acts of kindness that surprised these airmen. While others were beaten and starved, some were treated very well and their lives were saved by their enemy. These are stories that should be told. Most of those you will read about were not decorated for acts that seem to all of us extremely courageous; to them, they were just doing what was expected of them. Not one of the veterans interviewed for this book once mentioned medals or decorations. It was not part of their character.

I was extremely fortunate to locate witnesses in Europe and to find other archival documentation of events that occurred when these planes and airmen fell in occupied countries. I couldn't have done this without the enthusiastic support of some serious researchers in Poland, Austria, Italy, Croatia, Bulgaria and Slovakia. In some cases they had different views about the American experience in WWII and, in particular, concerning the air war over these countries. Despite the differences, these fine people spent countless hours searching records and finding and interviewing witnesses. Much of this is new information, not available until their research was completed. For a few of the veterans in these stories, it offered much more than new information; it offered closure. In one case, the new information may have provided new leads on what happened to the remains of a long-remembered loved one.

I was equally fortunate to be able to interview some of the European witnesses. I wouldn't have expected to see the outpouring of emotions as these people described, through tears, their thoughts and emotions as they saw lifeless American airmen around the crash site of their bomber, or how, years after the war ended, they took American military personnel to the site where six Americans "pilots" were buried.

Some of the stories you will read are lengthy; others are short. Some of the stories are more in-depth than others, in part because some of the experiences were longer than others. One experience in enemy territory lasted just a few hours, while others lasted a year. Some tell the story of the entire crew while others focus on individuals.

The stories are not incorporated into neat little packages. In some there are gaps. Others have inconsistencies from eyewitness statements recorded at that time. This isn't unusual, for we all see things through our own eyes, at different angles and from different perspectives. I haven't tried to make everything fit. Life doesn't work that way. One element the stories have in common is that they're all true and they're all about real people, good Americans.

At the end of each story of a bomber crew I've added what I have termed "The Story", which is background information of how the story came to be, including information about unusual and interesting events that occurred during the research and writing of the story. I hope you enjoy the stories. They're part of our rich history. Perhaps you can learn from them. I know I have.

WWII Europe.

Fallen Stars

There was no mistaking the impact the war had at home. There were daily reminders everywhere. Rationing was one of those reminders. Certain items weren't available anywhere and other items were rationed, requiring coupons. Victory Gardens sprang up in cities so people could grow their own fresh vegetables which weren't available in the stores.

Radio news stations told of the progress of the war. If one went to the movies for relaxation there were newsreels showing the latest developments in Europe and the Pacific. If there wasn't a bond drive, there were collections of old metal, rubber or other materials necessary for the war effort.

People in factories around the country made everything from munitions, to Spam, to steel helmets. There were blackouts along the coastlines to keep the enemy from having a clear view of America. One of the most noticeable reminders was the small number of young, able-bodied civilian men in most communities. Most of these young men were training for war or already fighting.

Patriotism reigned everywhere. America was proud of the job the young Americans were doing overseas. Families were also proud. To show their pride, signs with blue stars were hung in their windows, representing sons or daughters in service. Sadly, a gold star replaced the blue star when a loved one was killed in the war.

While the families were home worrying, the American boys fighting the war were trying to survive. They didn't want their families to worry. They wrote letters of reassurance and downplayed the dangerous business of fighting this war. When the boys knew they wouldn't return, their first thoughts were often of their families. Some of the airmen, while hanging in their parachutes descending rapidly into the unknown, recall thinking of their families and the Western Union telegram that would advise those at home that their son, husband, or brother was Missing in Action. At a time when the airmen needed every ounce of reserve for survival, their thoughts still turned to the impact this telegram would have on family. They would do everything in their power so the blue star hanging in the window at home wouldn't turn to gold. Some would succeed. Others wouldn't be so lucky.

The Boys from Venosa

Most of the Boys at Venosa, like other Americans fighting in Italy, did not know the details of the battle plans, much less the recent history of what had been occurring in Italy. Sure, they knew the main events, but most were unaware of the specifics leading up to these events. The details were left to the politicians and the generals while it was left to the young soldiers to do the fighting and dying, as it has always been throughout history. (**Author's Note:** Boys with a capital B is used specifically with reference to the airmen in the 485th Bomb Group.)

The stage was set for the invasion of Italy at the 10-day Casablanca conference in January of 1943, when Churchill and Roosevelt met and determined that they would impose "unconditional surrender" terms on all the Axis powers. They resolved to keep the momentum inspired by the recent Russian victories in the east and the rapid advances of the British 8th Army in North Africa. The Allies were not yet prepared to launch an invasion across the English Channel, but they did not want to lose momentum. After North Africa was conquered, the logical choice for the next step was Sicily and then to the mainland of Europe through Italy.

The Allies wasted little time and landings at Sicily began in early July. Benito Mussolini resigned his dictatorship in favor of Marshal Badoglio on July 25, 1943, just 15 days after Sicily was invaded by Canadian, American and British forces. In a radio broadcast, King Victor Emmanuel of Italy demanded the resignation of Mussolini, Il Duce. Some interesting circumstances led up to the radio broadcast.

Italy's Grand Council met for the purpose of discussing an urgent situation, the invasion of Sicily. Mussolini announced that he met with Hitler and Hitler refused to send any additional German troops to protect southern Italy from an Allied invasion. The Germans planned to leave southern Italy and establish defenses along the Po River in northern Italy. The Italians were being abandoned in the southern part of their country and Hitler demanded that Italian forces be moved north to reinforce German positions. Mussolini asked the council to accept Hitler's demand.

The members of the council could not believe their ears. They were being abandoned by Hitler, whom they had supported for years, their troops fighting side by side with his Afrika Corps. Dissension filled the room, in a setting where Mussolini had always received support. There was a call for a vote. Of the twenty-five members of the Grand Council, nineteen voted to reject Hitler's terms. Mussolini refused to accept the vote of the Council. The matter was presented to King Emmanuel, who couldn't bear to lose most of his country. The king, his guards by his side, confronted Mussolini and demanded his resignation. Mussolini was taken from his palace under guard and was ultimately detained in the Gran Sasso Hotel on Lake Bracciano. (He was later "rescued" from this "prison" by Germans.) His chief underlings were put under house arrest.

It was after Il Duce's arrest that King Emmanuel made his broadcast announcing Mussolini's replacement. During the radio broadcast, 73 year-old Marshal Pietro Badoglio's voice came on the air. Badoglio was known in earlier years as the commander who spearheaded the conquest of Ethiopia. In later years, he had not been so successful and was retired by Mussolini. He announced he was assuming control of the military government in Italy as Prime Minister and declared the war would continue against the Allies. Those who interfered would be "struck down without mercy". Badoglio displayed undying loyalty to his king. He would remain in control for 40 whole days! Protests immediately erupted in larger cities throughout Italy. The protestors demanded peace, while the Allies moved through Sicily.

Soon after gaining control, Badoglio directed subordinates to discreetly contact American and British diplomats at Vatican City, hoping to negotiate a peace with the Allies without giving up his position. Meanwhile, he recalled four divisions of Italian troops that were stationed in France and an additional 22 divisions from the Balkan countries, planning to shore up his defenses against the Allies. He continued to play both sides of the fence. Allied bombers stationed in North Africa and Sicily intensified air attacks on the Italian mainland, places like Bologna, Trento and Bolzano.

In secret negotiations, the Italians repeatedly refused to sign a surrender treaty, hoping for a better deal. Eisenhower held fast to his demand for unconditional surrender, ultimately giving Marshal Badoglio a 24-hour ultimatum. On September 3rd, several hours after the ultimatum, British forces crossed the Strait of Messina and landed on the Italian mainland, unopposed and welcomed by Italian rearguard troops. A few hours later Italian representatives signed the surrender document.

The official surrender was uneventful. It took place at Allied headquarters in Sicily with just a few present. Italian General Castellano signed the document for his country and General Walter Smith signed for the Allies. The Allies reserved the right to announce the surrender, awaiting the most favorable and opportune time for them.

Although the British landed on the mainland on September 3rd, the main invasion fleet was still several miles offshore, approaching Salerno, on September 8th. At 6:30 p.m., General Eisenhower announced the surrender. He made the announcement via United Nations radio, telling Italian troops and his own forces that the war between the Italians and Allies was over. Two additional messages were sent after Eisenhower's initial announcement. The first provided instructions to the Italian navy on how and where to surrender their ships, and the second was to the Italian people, ordering them to assist Allied troops and urging them to sabotage German operations. The British commander made a follow-up broadcast, issuing a demand for all Italian soldiers and airmen to surrender. Marshal Badoglio made a radio announcement from Rome, ordering his troops to cease hostilities against the Allies.

On the night of September 8th, the Allies began their mainland invasion at Salerno. German troops had replaced Italian forces and pitched battles were fought as the Americans struggled to keep a foothold on the mainland. The Allies held their ground, then moved forward. Throughout the remainder of the month battles raged. The British overran the airfields around Foggia. These bases and surrounding fields would play important roles as bases for the 15th Air Force heavy bombers. The B-24s and B-17s were now able to take the fight farther north, ultimately into the far reaches of Poland and as far north as Berlin.

The British 8th Army fought their way up the east side of Italy, while the American 5th Army fought its war on the west side. This was the way it would remain throughout the war. Both armies encountered fierce resistance.

The Italians may have surrendered, but the Germans still occupied most of the country. Hitler's master plan may have been to fall back to northern Italy, but the Germans would fight every

1. 485th BG Headquarters, formerly a farmhouse

2. A Venosa lavatory, with Jack Llewellyn, Les Klopp and Pete Venson washing up

step of the way as they retreated. It would be more than a year before the Allies would reach the Germans' final line of defense in northern Italy. In October 1943, Marshal Badoglio declared war on Germany, a meaningless gesture. As soon as the area around Foggia was secured, the 15th Air Force began planning operations for its B-17 and B-24 heavy bombers from the recently captured airfields in the region. The first combat missions of the heavy bombers were flown from Italy on November 2, 1943.

The first heavy bombers in Italy were brought up from North Africa. Two were B-24 groups and four were B-17 groups. New groups, formed and trained in the United States, began to arrive. Temporary bases were being constructed as quickly as possible across the Foggia Plain by American and British engineers. These were not bases with

7

concrete runways and hangars. They were carved from wheat fields and orchards, then covered with Pierced Steel Planking (PSP). In most cases the bombers were repaired on their hardstands, in open weather. The largest building on a base was often a farmhouse or headquarters building made from tufa blocks.

Most of the boys had no dormitories or barracks. They slept on cots in tents, which were hot and stuffy in the Italian summer and cold, damp and miserable in the winter. They washed themselves in metal helmets filled with cold water. They ate powdered eggs for breakfast, complimenting the powdered milk they drank.

The winter of 1944-1945 would be one of the coldest in modern European history, with heavy snowfall. There were no sidewalks at the bases near Foggia, so the wet winter conditions were miserable. The airmen were here to fly and they and their equipment were ill-prepared for the thick mud, which engulfed their feet and shoes. Tents leaked or collapsed from the snow. The men made makeshift stoves from oil drums or other materials, using 88mm shell casings for the chimneys and fighter drop tanks to store the 100 octane gasoline that fueled the stoves. The tents had makeshift floors at best, made from straw mats, scrap wood, pieces of Pierced Steel Planking, tufa block or whatever could be scrounged, stolen or bartered.

The Boys who repaired and maintained the planes had it the worst. At most bases they did all their work outside, including engine changes, regardless of weather conditions. Whether it was freezing cold or stifling hot, even in the snow and rain, they had to keep the planes flying for that next mission.

Is it any wonder there was some resentment (most of it good-natured) toward those "other" bomber guys in England, in the 8th Air Force? Newsreels depicted them as living in Quonset huts, dormitories, even in castles. They had real beds, indoor plumbing (or so the rumors went) and some had running water in their quarters. It was rumored they had real eggs for breakfast and had real milk to drink.

3. Charles Neer, Jim Sharpe and Stuart Gansell, 830th B.S.

4. Wayne Whiting, 831st B.S. gunner, at the squadron outhouse

5. Al Trinche, 828th B.S. bombardier, in front of his Italian home

6. 828th B.S. tent area

7. Maintenance in the winter could be difficult. The plane is *LIFE*, 830th B.S.

8. The Red Cross supplies refreshments on the flight line, summer of 1944

9. Lt. Colonel Douglas Cairns, final 485th C.O. at bat in April 1945

They even had movie stars flying with them, such as Jimmy Stewart and Clark Gable. It seems that people were always talking about the 8th Air Force. There were always news reports about them. They seemed to get a lot of visits from the big stars, according to those reports. You didn't see many big name reporters coming to Italy for their stories. Most preferred better accommodations.

In England, the boys went sightseeing to places like London and Cambridge, taking trains or other public transportation to get there. They visited famous places like the London Bridge, Buckingham Palace and Westminster Abbey, places they had heard and read about. The boys in Italy hitchhiked on dusty or muddy roads, hoping a British or American army truck would stop. Their destination might be Bari or Foggia. The history here was unfamiliar to most G.I.s, except for some of the main attractions in places like Rome, Florence or Venice, which were still in German hands when the boys arrived in Italy. A day of hitchhiking might get them to Bari where they would walk around for an hour or so, then end up at the Red Cross center to have a donut and a cup of coffee. This was a sightseeing tour in Italy. Occasionally, some of the pilots flew a few of the boys to a base near the coast where they could go swimming for a few hours.

Some of the groups located places for the boys to spend a few days at temporary rest camps away from the base. These places generally weren't fancy or luxurious, but they were getaways. Some of the boys who flew combat went to the Isle of Capri after they had completed about half of their missions. A typical stay was five to seven days. Capri was a beautiful island, several miles off the coast from Naples. They had great accommodations in good hotels, with real beds with sheets on them. They had running water and could bathe as often as they wished, with warm water. They had good food and there was even night life. There was sightseeing, swimming and spectacular scenery. This was a one-time experience, a reward for living, so to speak.

Those who didn't fly did not fare as well. They weren't allowed to go to Capri. Rome, just 200 miles north of Venosa, was captured by the Allies in June of 1944 and some went there. Non-flying officers occasionally went to Villagio Mancuso, a resort along the southern coast of Italy. The non-flying boys didn't fare as well in other aspects, either. They were overseas for the duration of the war. There was no end in sight for them. They seldom complained about that particular aspect. They knew they would eventually get to go home and their buddies who flew combat might never make it back.

The boys in England found people with whom they could communicate, people who spoke English (well, sort of). The boys in England could get dates with girls who spoke English, a rarity in Italy. The female companionship available in Italy was often a teenage prostitute, offered by a pre-teenage boy whose only knowledge of the English language seemed to be a few words like "G.I., you go boom-boom with my sister?"

After the war, it was argued that some of the resentment was due to the glory and attention the 8th Air Force boys in England received from the news media. It really wasn't that. The boys in Italy realized there was no glory in war. They knew that the bitter, bone-chilling cold at high altitude was the same. It didn't matter whether the fighter attacks and the flak-filled skies were over Vienna, Ploesti, Berlin, Nuremberg or Blechhammer. It looked and felt the same, as well as the gut-wrenching emotions when seeing a buddy's bomber burst into flames, with no parachutes coming out. The death, terror and destruction were the same, no matter where it occurred. That's why most of the teasing was good-natured. It was just the living conditions that were different, and some of that may have been propaganda back at home, trying to show that the boys who were dying every day really lived pretty well.

The bomber bases in Italy materialized near towns and villages with names like Manduria, San Pancrazio, San Giovanni, Castelluccio, Cerignola, Pantanella and Spinazzola. The names were difficult to spell and more difficult to pronounce correctly. There would eventually be twenty-one heavy bomb groups in the 15th Air Force (fifteen B-24 groups and six B-17 groups). The last heavy bomb group assigned to the 15th Air Force was the 485th Bomb Group, based near Venosa. Like the other units, they were temporary. They began setting up their tents in April 1944 and their base was disbanded before the European war officially ended.

The Boys at Venosa knew little about the history of their surroundings. The people were poor and the Boys wondered if this was the way it had always been, or whether it was a result of the Fascist regime in Italy. They didn't know Venosa had once been a thriving city or that a couple of centuries before the birth of Christ, Venosa had been one of the most important towns in

Italy, on the road to Rome. They weren't aware that one of the greatest of the Latin poets, Horace, was born in Venosa. They also didn't know that Venosa had been conquered by the Byzantines, the Saracens and the Normans. Now the Allies were here, but just temporarily. They too would leave, as had the other conquering forces.

Little remains today to indicate that for a very brief period in the history of the world, more than 2500 Americans lived outside of Venosa. Even before the European war was officially over, the 485th had packed up and left, taking their tents and most traces of their existence with them. The remaining planes were scrapped and the Pierced Steel Planking that made up the runway was removed, returning the land to its pastoral setting.

The 485th left its mark though, in bombing raids over targets like Ploesti, Vienna, Blechhammer, Munich and Linz. The marks are no longer visible in most of these places. The only visible marks remaining are in places like Neupre, St. Avold, Nettuno, Carthage and Florence. The marks are white crosses and Stars of David, carefully arranged in neat rows and on stone monuments in American military cemeteries. More than 470 Boys from this group were killed in WWII. Other groups which had experienced combat longer had even greater losses. Other marks remain, but they are invisible. These are the marks the 485th Bomb Group and the other 20 heavy bomb groups in Italy left on the world, and the vital role they played in bombing the industrial might out of Germany.

The Boys of the 485th were unaware of the big picture or the world situation. There were few radios. They heard about the big battles like Iwo Jima, Okinawa and the Battle of the Bulge. They were participants in some of the big aerial battles. They knew how many missions they'd flown and how many they had left to complete their tour of duty. As with most boys their age, they weren't really too concerned with the specifics of politics. They knew they were fighting against madmen like Hitler and

Mussolini and they just wanted to finish their job and go home. They knew Venosa was a temporary place for them, regardless of what happened. They expected to finish their 35 sorties or 50 missions and return to what their orders called the Z.I., the Zone of Interior. In civilian terms, this was the good old USA.

Many kept up on the scores and standings of their favorite baseball or football teams. Mail was an important commodity to most and they read and reread their letters. That's how they got their news from home. They wrote to girlfriends, wives, family and friends. They occasionally played baseball or football when they weren't flying and they went to the Enlisted Mens Club or Officers Club to have a few drinks or gamble. They didn't always have their choice of liquor, so they had to settle for whatever was available. It seemed that "Gin and Juice" was usually available. They could attend movies, which were originally shown outside at night, before a multi-use building was constructed. There was an occasional USO show, but the big stars didn't come to Venosa. The Boys worked at making their tents as comfortable as possible. If the flying weather was good, they could be back in the U.S. in 4 or 5 months, if all went well. Unfortunately, not all would be so lucky. This is their story.

Friends and Foes

Aside from being killed or seriously injured, the thing many airmen dreaded the most was being shot down in enemy territory. This was something for which they had little preparation or training. Most hadn't bailed out before and while they had received some instruction on how to bail out, few had actually jumped out of an airplane.

The other option, sometimes available if the plane wasn't damaged too badly or on fire, was landing the aircraft or ditching in the water. Landing required a fairly flat piece of land to set the plane down, something not available over the mountainous terrain of much of southern and central Europe. The B-24 tended to break up when ditched in the water and sank quickly. The bomber's ditching characteristics were well-known among the airmen and few chose this option if any other was available.

Some of the airmen carried .45 caliber pistols. Some squadrons and groups required them to carry the pistols on missions; others made it optional. In most cases downed airmen found the guns of little use. The airmen attended no survival schools and had little training on how to escape and evade. Some recall receiving lectures on survival in enemy territory, but others don't remember any such training aside from being warned to stay away from civilians in Germany and Austria, where the most fervent Nazis were located. Stories circulated about flyers who were beaten to death by angry civilians after they parachuted or crash-landed near a target they had just bombed.

Many had heard they would receive the best treatment if they were captured by the Luftwaffe. Stories of SS atrocities circulated at their bases, so the airmen were encouraged to avoid capture by the SS or Gestapo, although they had little choice in the matter. There was little chance to evade capture in Germany. There were great distances to travel in order to reach Allied lines, until the last couple months of the war when Allied advances were rapid. For these reasons, evasions in Germany were almost non-existent and evasions through Austria were uncommon.

Evasions from Romania, Bulgaria, and Greece were also difficult. The difficulty of the terrain and the distances to Allied territory made for an almost impossible journey. Evasions through Poland, Czechoslovakia and Hungary were not common, but became more frequent as the war progressed and the Russians approached from the east.

The best chances for evasion, statistically, were from northern Italy and Yugoslavia, particularly from Yugoslavia. The Italian Partisans aided Americans on many occasions and Italian civilians, especially in those rural areas, were often friendly and hid the American flyers.

The best chances for evasion were from and through Yugoslavia, where both the Chetniks and Partisans were forces to be reckoned with. A civil war was raging in this country even while the Germans were occupiers. There were four primary factions the American airmen had to deal with if shot down over Yugoslavia. The first faction was the German Army. The Germans occupied the major cities and were in force, to varying degrees, in the more rural areas.

The Germans were assisted by the pro-German forces, the Ustashe or Ustashi. The Ustashe were known for their atrocities, torture and brutal treatment of anyone not in agreement with them. If an airman was captured by the Ustashe he could expect to be killed. When the Italians entered the southern part of Yugoslavia they put Ante Pavelic in charge of the Ustashe. He was considered by some to be even more racist than Adolf Hitler and it is estimated that he had hundreds of thousands of Serbs, Jews and Gypsies in Croatia killed.[1]

The Chetniks were supporters of the Yugoslavian government in exile. Draza Mihailovic was an officer in the army until the Germans and other Axis powers entered Yugoslavia. He then retreated into the mountains. A Serb, he was appointed National Defense Minister by the government in exile. He had few supplies and his troop numbers were small. His followers were organized into small groups of fighters near some of the villages. Although he claimed the groups were under his command, in reality he didn't have complete control over them. The aim of the Chetniks was to maintain the status quo, to return Yugoslavia to its pre-war status under the king with the Serbs in control. Croats, Muslims and Slovenians were generally not allowed to join the Chetniks. The Chetniks received the support of the British in the early years of the war and concentrated most of their efforts in Serbia.

Josip Broz, more commonly known as Tito, was the Partisan commander. As a communist, he received aid from the Russians. Tito was part-Serb and part-Croat and he welcomed the various factions into his group with the common cause of driving the Germans out of Yugoslavia.

In December 1943 at the Tehran conference, the Allies decided to provide support equally to the Partisans and Chetniks. By the summer of 1944 all of the supplies were being sent to the Partisans, virtually insuring the Partisans of victory over the Chetniks in Yugoslavia. For both the Chetniks and the Partisans, getting the Germans out of their country was secondary to gaining control of their own people by defeating their adversaries within.

Downed American airmen were thrown into this volatile situation. If found by the Ustashe, they would be killed or captured. The Germans would most likely send them to a POW camp. In most cases when found by either the Partisans or the Chetniks, they would be hidden and safely returned to Italy.

In the Adriatic Sea, off the coast of Yugoslavia, was the island of Vis. The island was held by the Partisans and provided an emergency landing strip, a safe haven for damaged Allied planes. If airmen from the 485th made it to Vis they could be assured of an early return to Italy. Many of the flyers were trying to make it to Vis when they bailed out over the Yugoslavian mainland. Late in the war, a field near Zara, along the northwest coast of Yugoslavia, was also used as an emergency landing strip when it was firmly in the hands of the Partisans.

NOTES AND REFERENCES

[1] Franklin Lindsay, *Beacons in the Night*, pg. 21

I'm So Glad He Asked Me To Dance

June 9th would be a sad day for the Boys in the 485th, although they didn't know this as they were briefed on the target, Munich. They listened quietly to the briefing. Ultimately, they would lose five aircraft and 50 crewmen that day, most to fighters. This is the story of one of those lost crews.

At home, "Long Ago and Far Away" was at the top of the record charts. A world record litter of puppies (23) was born to Lena, a foxhound, in Ambler, Pennsylvania. In Europe, the Normandy invasion had taken place three days earlier and the beachheads were secured. Bayeux, five miles inland from the French coast, had been liberated the day before. In Italy, the American 5th Army was now thirty-two miles north of Rome. This would be the day that Premier Badoglio, Mussolini's replacement would resign, but it had no impact on the airmen or the other Allied forces fighting in Italy.

Jim McNulty's crew had trained together in Fairmont, Nebraska with the other original crews, before going overseas. They were part of the 831st Squadron. While in Nebraska, they had gotten to know each other fairly well. Jim McNulty and his wife

Jessie had gotten married in November 1943, as the group was being formed.[1]

Eugene Maylath, the copilot, was from New York. The navigator, Ormiston Brown and his wife were from New Mexico. Ed Lubanovich, the bombardier, and his wife Yolanda were from Ohio. Robert Irmen, the ball gunner, was from Minnesota. The nose gunner, Lawrence Miller and his wife were from Indiana.

Eugene Brittin, the top turret gunner, was from New Jersey. He was small, mild-mannered and easygoing, with flaxen hair. Alfred Bertelli, the flight engineer, was from Massachusetts. Bertelli didn't drink or smoke and was a serious, although fun-loving member of the crew.

10. Lt. James McNulty crew, 831st B.S. photo taken in Nebraska. Standing, left to right: Jim McNulty, pilot; Ed Lubanovich, bombardier; Ormiston Brown, navigator, and Eugene Maylath, copilot. Middle row, left to right: Eugene Brittin, top turret; Lawrence Griggs, radio operator/waist gunner; Al Bertelli, flight engineer/waist gunner; Robert Irmen, ball gunner, and Murray Sheridan, tail gunner. Seated in front: Lawrence Miller, nose gunner.

Lawrence Griggs, from Los Angeles, was the radio operator. He was known as a tough little scrapper, someone who wouldn't back down. It was rumored that his girlfriend had been attacked by five guys one night when he was with her. Griggs grabbed her and they took off in his '35 Ford, with four of the attackers hanging on to the side of the car. The four thugs were crushed when the car struck another object. No one knew for certain if it was true, but Griggs wasn't a guy to mess with. He was a welcome addition to the combat crew.

The original tail gunner, Murray Sheridan, had been seriously wounded by flak May 22nd, on a mission to northern Italy. He was replaced by Walter Lindsey from Shreveport, Louisiana.[2]

Prior to going overseas, the crew gathered regularly on weekends with Ed and Yolanda Lubanovich. Already an "old" married couple approaching their mid 20's, they welcomed the crew into their home, where Yolanda became popular for the spaghetti dinners she cooked for the entire crew each Saturday night.[3]

Ed and Yolanda first met at a dance in Lorain, Ohio in March of 1941. The big, husky Lubanovich saw Yolanda sitting at a table. For both of them it was the first time at this club. He approached her and asked her to dance. She accepted and they started dancing. His next comment as they danced was, "Are you Catholic?" She responded, "Yes", and asked why. He answered saying, "My wife has to be Catholic. I'm going to marry you." She loved the way he danced. He was a wonderful dancer, so graceful as they moved across the floor and

11.W.D. "Jack" Lindsey, who replaced Murray Sheridan as tail gunner, after Sheridan was seriously wounded.

23

12. Ed and Yolanda Lubanovich, the day after their wedding (July 1943 photo)

they became inseparable after this dance. Within three months she was wearing his ring and they were married in 1943, while Ed was still an aviation cadet.

The crew named their plane *The Character*, at Murray Sheridan's suggestion. The ten airmen on the crew were all characters and their plane was the 11th character. The name stuck and was eventually painted on the side of the plane. After Sheridan's combat injuries he was hospitalized in Bari, Italy before he was sent back to the U.S. for a long, painful recuperation.[4]

The Boys were upset on June 9th to learn their plane wasn't

13. Arcade photos, left to right: Jessie and Jim McNulty; Jessie McNulty and Yolanda Lubanovich, and Jim McNulty and Ed Lubanovich.

available. They were assigned another plane and weren't at all happy about it as they had come to rely on their plane. There was some grumbling before the mission started, but all that stopped after take-off. For most of the crew, it was their thirteenth mission.

The various groups formed up and headed for Germany. One of the other groups was 15 minutes late, delaying the formation. Due to this error, they missed their rendezvous with their fighter escorts and headed for a heavily defended target in Germany without their "Little Friends" to escort them.[5]

The formation was flying at 23,500 feet and as they approached the I.P. (Initial Point), the generators went out on McNulty's aircraft and the turrets became inoperable.[6] The intercom system also failed. Other airmen in the group watched the bomber as it dropped its landing gear, pulled out of the formation and made a 180 degree turn to the left, reversing its course and releasing its bombs as it turned. There was no fighter escort to pick them up on their way south and without the functioning turrets, they were an easy target for any enemy fighters that spotted them.[7]

Joe South, a gunner in another B-24 flying off the right wing of McNulty's plane, reported the following:

Lt. McNulty, who was flying to our left, dropped his landing gear and made a 180 degree turn to the left and released his bombs at the same time. This was about five minutes before the I.P. and when last seen four fighters were on his tail. I could not see if they were firing at him but all four engines were running and there was no smoke from the plane.[8]

Another 831st gunner, Ray Heskes, in Lt. Phelts' plane, also saw what was happening.

I was flying in the number two position of the low box, first wave. From the lower ball turret I saw Lt. McNulty as he banked to the left with landing gear down. As far as I know, no fighters attacked him. He went into the clouds below us with control of his ship. All four engines seemed to be in good order. There were two P-51's below me and they might have escorted him; although I could not say for sure.[9]

For whatever reasons, the German fighters seen by South and others did not attack McNulty's plane and the fighters seen by Heskes did not escort the stricken bomber.

Without the intercom system, communication with those in the back of McNulty's plane was impossible. Tension filled the air as McNulty and Maylath flew their bomber south, over the mountain peaks. The thick clouds provided cover for the plane, hiding them from any German fighters in the area. The men were freezing because there was no electricity for their heated flying suits. Bertelli, the flight engineer, came forward in the plane and contacted the pilots. McNulty instructed him to gather the gunners in the rear of the plane and to bail out if they saw the bomb bay doors opening. The opening of the doors would be the signal to bail out. There was no point for the gunners to remain in their turrets at this point, since the turrets weren't working. They couldn't defend themselves from a fighter attack.

The gunners in the rear of the plane left their turrets and assembled in the waist, at the entrance to the bomb bay. Lubanovich and Miller left their stations in the nose and crawled through the small passage to the flight deck behind the pilots. The bomber made it over the highest peaks in Austria and continued south into Italy. Shortly after they crossed the border into Italy they lost the protection of the clouds and a German fighter found them, attacking from below.

Friedrich Scheer, a German pilot in the 8th Staffel of III Gruppe of JG53 had taken off that morning from his base at Maniago. He was patrolling the area north of Pordenone in his ME 109 fighter when he spotted a lone B-24 bomber at 1125 hours, local time. He attacked the B-24. It would be his eleventh victory and an easy one.[10]

Irmen, the ball gunner, was killed instantly in the attack, hit by a cannon shell as the aircraft burst into flames. Lindsey was wounded in the leg. McNulty opened the bomb bay doors. Miller was standing at the rear of the flight deck at the front entrance to the bomb bay. Lubanovich, standing behind him, pushed him out and immediately followed. Brittin, Griggs and Lindsey bailed out through the camera/escape hatch shortly after an explosion rocked the plane. There was another major explosion just after they bailed out.

Lubanovich and Miller made it to the ground, separately but safely, just outside of Cordovado. Both were immediately captured by German soldiers. Lubanovich was surrounded by Italian workers in the vineyard when he landed. The workers, armed with pitchforks, appeared unfriendly, and Lubanovich was actually relieved when German SS soldiers arrived on the scene.

Some of the locals witnessed the event from the ground.[11] Rosino Biason was working for a family in Cordovado. She saw an American bomber appear overhead and it flew east over the village, with pieces of the airplane falling off. It disappeared after two parachutes came out of the plane. The villagers ran to the center of town. Biason watched as German soldiers dragged one of the airmen to the village square.

Brittin, hanging in his parachute, looked around and saw a parachute some distance away, descending slowly. He looked down and saw a body falling. As he watched in horror, the body hit the ground, the parachute failing to open. Brittin looked around, but his plane was out of sight. In the distance, he saw a column of smoke rising, a sure sign the airplane had crashed.

Mrs. Alugia Pizzolitto was in the village of Villanova-Malafesta when she saw the bomber coming in her direction. She saw a man fall from the plane. His parachute didn't open as he fell and he landed in an open field. Local villagers rushed to him, but he was dead. Pizzolitto watched as another airman landed in his parachute about 100 meters away.

Gino and Nevio Biason were just boys living on a nearby farm when they saw the bomber approach Villanova-Malafesta. It was smoking and the engines were roaring and sputtering. It was flying so low that the boys feared it would crash into the village. The B-24 was just a few meters above the rooftops. Pieces were falling off the plane as it flew overhead. They saw the big bomber explode and a wing and an engine flew off just before the plane crashed near the Tagliamento River. There were flames and smoke everywhere. The boys were about 200 meters from the crash.

Gino and some other boys ran to the crash site. They saw pieces of aircraft all around them. Gino found a pair of machineguns with a seat attached to them and hid them in a cornfield.

Margherita Trevisan was nearby and saw people running from the village to the crash site. The plane had crashed on the opposite side of a tributary of the river, so people got in boats to get nearer. One of the women saw an airman run out of the burning fuselage. He was engulfed in flames. The woman beat out the flames, but the airman died. She tried to get closer to the burning plane, but the heat and flames kept her away. She saw the bodies of two men burning in the plane. She returned to the dead airman and saw that his watch and ring had been taken by some of the villagers. German soldiers arrived shortly and restored order to the scene.

The dead airmen were buried in the cemetery at Villanova later that same afternoon. The entire area was scattered with pieces of wreckage, large and small.

Brittin landed safely. Nearby he spotted one of the Boys who had bailed out with him. He approached the injured airman and saw it was Lawrence Griggs. Griggs was severely injured, with an obvious broken leg and other leg injuries. By process of elimination Brittin realized the parachute that hadn't opened must belong to the new tail gunner, the only other crewman in the rear of the plane. Brittin didn't even know his name. It was Lindsey.

Griggs was in bad shape and in a lot of pain. Brittin took the morphine from his escape kit and injected Griggs with a syrette. Three German soldiers arrived as Brittin tended to his friend in the field. The Germans searched them and took their escape kits and other items. Seeing that Griggs was severely wounded, an Italian doctor was summoned to the scene. Brittin showed the doctor the empty morphine syrette. The doctor gave Griggs another shot, then set his broken leg and put a splint on it.

A crowd of Italians gathered around the two airmen in the field. Gino Biason was one of those in the crowd. He couldn't get too close to the airmen, but could see one of them had a serious leg wound. He heard from others that the airman's foot was missing, but he didn't know if that was true.

About 30 minutes later, an old Italian truck arrived and Griggs was loaded into the back. Brittin was told Griggs was being taken to the hospital. Griggs was taken to the hospital at Portogruaro, several kilometers away, where he died the next day.[12]

Brittin was taken to a farmhouse at St. Michele al Tagliamento where he was questioned by the German soldiers.[13] He gave them his name, rank and serial number. The Germans continued to question him about such things as his unit and the target. They didn't get anywhere with their questioning. One of the questions asked was how many women were on the plane. These Germans and their propaganda! They had probably been told they were winning the war and the Americans had resorted to having women do the fighting.

During the evening a single guard was assigned to Brittin and the other Germans went to other parts of the house. During the night, something happened that caused the Germans to go outside, but they returned and went to sleep as Brittin pondered his future. About 5:00 the next morning he had to use the toilet, so he went outside. He was surprised to see that there was no guard posted, so he kept going. Knowing he was in northern Italy, Brittin headed south across the rugged countryside.

Within a couple of hours he came across some Italians who appeared friendly. Through sign language he was able to get a fair idea of his location. He decided to hide for the day, knowing he could easily be spotted and identified. Late in the day he got

up and headed east, towards Trieste. He met an Italian boy with a rowboat, and the boy took him across the Tagliamento River. The boy then took him home, where he was given a meal by the boy's family. Here he obtained civilian clothes so he wouldn't be so conspicuous.

The Italian boy had an English grammar book and, word by word, pointing to one word at a time, they were able to communicate. Brittin learned that three British soldiers were in the area and they would come to see him in the night. Around 8:00 in the evening, a South African soldier, who had escaped from a POW camp appeared. He took Brittin to another home in the area where he and two other South Africans were staying.

14. Eugene Brittin, before going overseas

Brittin was lucky. He was at the farm of Luigi Nicodemo, in the hamlet of Paludo, about two kilometers from Latisana.[14] Luigi's family lived on the farm, along with his elderly father, Giuseppe. Umberto D'Olivo and his wife and five daughters were recent additions at the farm. Umberto was a successful businessman in the area. Umberto and his family lived in Latisana until mid-May of 1944, when the village was bombed on the 19th by the Americans. Umberto moved his family into the country to keep them safe from the bombers.

D'Olivo had four or five employees at his business in Latisana, selling food and livestock. He got along well with the German occupiers and the Italian fascists, a necessity for a businessman. What the Germans didn't know was D'Olivo was hiding a South

15. Umberto and Caterina D'Olivo

African officer by the name of Greenburg, an escapee from a nearby POW camp. Greenburg moved with the family to the farm on May 19th. Several other escapees joined them and the farm was well-organized by the time Brittin arrived. The escapees worked in the fields in the daytime helping Nicodemo with farming.

Brittin became ill after his arrival and stayed in this "safe house" for almost a month. After his recovery, he was told by the D'Olivo's that Partisans would bring a truck "on Saturday" for him and his South African companions.

They waited and waited. After several Saturdays had passed, they were still hopeful that the truck would come the next Saturday. Nearly two months later, at the end of August, Brittin decided to set off on his own, heading for Trieste. While walking, he found more friendly Italians and was taken to the Partisan headquarters in the area. He waited there ten more days for a truck. Here he met up with some British evadees. The small group left together, headed back in the same direction Brittin had come. Brittin decided to stop at Nicodemo's farmhouse. The South Africans were still hiding out there, so he made the decision to remain with them.

Meanwhile, a plot was unfolding nearby. A young Italian was smitten with Maria, the eldest daughter of Umberto D'Olivo, by all accounts a beautiful young woman. The Italian apparently heard that some Allies were hidden at the farm. When Maria rejected his advances, he became spiteful and decided to retaliate. He contacted the SS detachment in nearby Conegliano and told them that Allied soldiers were being hidden at the farm.

The next day Brittin was in a nearby field when German SS troops arrived. There must have been an adequate warning system because most of the people at the farm escaped, apparently seeing the German truck driving up the road. Not all of them got away. The women and children stayed at the farm. The SS captured Umberto's wife, Caterina, and Luigi's sister-in-law, Carolina Tecli, and a servant. They were taken to a prison camp near Padova. The SS troopers ransacked the house and burned it to the ground. Brittin thought the South Africans were captured.

The SS searched for Maria in town but didn't locate her. Umberto escaped arrest because he was in the hospital that day. Caterina was later released, due to the efforts of an Italian general. Carolina was released at the end of the war. The D'Olivo girls went to live with grandparents and the Nicodemos left the area. The two Italian families paid a high price for their kindness to the Allies.

Again Brittin left on foot, hiding and walking for a few days, not knowing who he could trust. One day while hiking down a country road, he saw a man coming toward him. The man was Pietro Basei. Brittin decided to take a chance and approached the

16. The D'Olivo sisters after WWII

man. He explained he was an American and Pietro understood and took Brittin home with him.[15]

Basei and his neighbor, Antonio Presotto, shared a common courtyard. Presotto and Basei talked it over and decided to help Brittin. Brittin got lucky again. Germans were all around and it was extremely dangerous for these Italians to hide an American. During the day Brittin hid in an outbuilding, a straw barn, coming out to stretch only in the evenings. It was impossible to get past the Piave River due to the heavy concentration of German troops in the area, so Brittin had to wait. For several months his guardians hid him.

After six months, a New Zealander in the area was able to get Brittin to a PT boat. Along with twelve Evadees (eleven New Zealanders and one South African) who were hiding nearby, he made it to the coast and was evacuated by PT boat to Ancona, Italy on March 17, 1945. This was more than nine months after his initial capture. The other men had been POWs since earlier in the war, captured in North Africa. When Italy signed the armistice with the Allies, they were released. Before the Germans could round them up, they fled to the countryside and had been hiding out since September 1943. It was a Catholic priest by the name of Augustino who put Brittin in touch with the New Zealander who, in turn, facilitated the return to Allied territory.

Brittin was not in good shape when he was returned to Allied hands. He was debriefed and sent home almost immediately, where he was hospitalized. The Boys back at Venosa were not told of his return.

Lubanovich and Miller were taken to POW camps. Lubanovich was placed in solitary confinement for six weeks after his capture. Eventually he went to Stalag Luft III.

After the Boys went down, the families back at home received telegrams from the War Department telling them their sons, brothers and husbands were Missing in Action.[16] Yolanda Lubanovich lived with her parents in Ohio. She noted they were acting strangely quiet one day when she came home for lunch. Further inquiry revealed that a telegram had arrived. She was shocked and overwhelmed. Yolanda and a sister of Ed's went to give Ed's mother the unfortunate news. She was devastated by the news. Shortly thereafter, she went downstairs, sat down, and had a heart attack and stroke.

Yolanda later received confirmation that Ed was a POW and got a letter from him. In fact, she received a few letters, the last one dated December 13, 1944. She was mailed regular newsletters from the Red Cross about POWs. As the months rolled by the newsletter had articles alluding to the mistreatment of the American POWs in Germany. Worried sick, she lost weight, at one point weighing only 85 lbs.

With the Russians approaching from the east in late January, the POWs from Stalag Luft III were evacuated from their camp. After walking through the snow and riding in crowded boxcars with multiple stops along the route, they made their way to Nurnberg, where they witnessed the devastation of Allied air raids. Much of their time was spent in foxholes they had dug to protect themselves from "friendly" bombs. Finally in April, they left for a camp at Moosberg on foot, a trip that would last several days. About the same time Miller was also released from his POW camp.

The POWs arrived at Moosberg on April 13th. The camp was overcrowded with thousands of Allied POWs. The POWs slept in big tents, on straw on the ground or in hastily dug foxholes. Allied bombings continued in the area, with medium bombers attacking the smaller targets. Lubanovich and the other survivors were liberated by the U.S. Army on April 29th, when General Patton himself appeared in the camp.

Yolanda Lubanovich waited impatiently, listening to news broadcasts, hoping Ed had survived. On May 29th she received a telegram from the Red Cross, advising her that Ed was in American hands. There were still no specific details about him or his condition.

A few days later she received a telegram from Ed saying he had arrived in the States. He gave her instructions to meet him at the train station in Cleveland, on a specific date and time, to come alone, and not tell anyone.

After receiving the telegram, she got a phone call from Bill Moos, who trained with Ed. Moos went overseas to Italy with a different group and had also been a POW. He had been in the same POW camp as Ed and had last seen him at Camp Lucky Strike at Le Havre, France. Moos wasn't aware that Yolanda received a telegram from Ed. He cautioned Yolanda to be prepared for how Ed looked, telling her she would not recognize him due to weight loss and other changes in appearance. Relieved he was coming home but also apprehensive, Yolanda didn't know what to expect. She had sent her big, healthy husband off to war and didn't know what she was going to get back.

She was excited, but also confused and troubled about the prospect of not recognizing Ed in a crowded train station full of G.I.s. Yolanda was working in a factory and she told two of her good friends about Ed's arrival date. She expressed her concern about not recognizing him. Her friends, Betty Jane and Noreen, sympathized with her. Betty Jane had grown up with Ed, living across the street from him and had known Ed as a thin, gangly boy. She made a proposal that she and Noreen accompany Yolanda to the train station. Betty Jane was sure she would recognize Ed. She and Noreen would be in a location where they could see people get off the train. When she spotted Ed, she would point him out to Yolanda. Yolanda agreed, still uncertain as to what to expect.

On the appointed day, Yolanda borrowed her brother's car to drive to Cleveland, accompanied by her two companions. Betty Jane and Noreen found a good observation point at the train station while Yolanda waited on the platform. The train arrived and the passengers began exiting. The train was full of soldiers. Yolanda looked over at her friends and she wondered how

17. Yolanda and a much thinner Ed
Lubanovich, shortly after Ed's return home
(June 1945 photo)

anyone could spot him in the crowd. Suddenly Betty Jane waved and pointed to a tall, thin, gray-haired soldier exiting the train, and then she and Noreen disappeared into the crowd. The two took a bus home so that Ed and Yolanda could be alone.

Was this her man? As he approached she knew it was him, 50 lbs. lighter and prematurely gray from malnutrition, but it was her Ed. Their eyes met and they embraced, quietly. Finally, in a soft voice he said, "I didn't think I'd ever see you again."

No other words were needed. They slowly walked to the car, holding hands. She thought of the date, June 9th, exactly one year after he was shot down.

Ed didn't speak as they drove through Cleveland, still holding hands. Would he be OK? Could he ever put this horrible experience behind him? It was awkward. Should she say something? What could she say? They both remained quiet.

He drove along the lake road, toward Lorain. Yolanda was surprised when Ed turned into the parking lot of a restaurant and dance hall. "The White Oaks" was a place they frequented before he left. They walked in and sat down, still holding hands. For a while there was no conversation. Then he leaned over and asked, almost shyly, "Would you like to dance?" As they moved across the dance floor, there was no need for words. He communicated by his movements, gracefully, holding her passionately. It would be OK. Once again, she was glad he asked her to dance.

Yolanda never told Ed about the conspiracy with her friends at the train station. Good friends can keep good secrets for the right reasons.

Many of the families hadn't received confirmation that their loved ones were POWs. For them, the waiting was even more agonizing. Some of the wives kept in touch. Yolanda received several letters from Jessie McNulty, pilot James McNulty's wife. In early June Yolanda received one such letter. Jessie relayed information she received in a letter from Brittin's parents, saying it was rumored that five Americans were found in the plane after it crashed.

June 2, 1945

Dear Yolanda,[17]

Well, I am certainly a nervous wreck and so if this letter sounds mixed up you'll know why. Yolanda, I hope I am not boring you but I hope you understand no matter what Eddy can add to this good or bad will help because we have to know the truth no matter what it is. I am going to try and stick out next week in work and then I may have to take some time off because I am so nervous and upset.

I hope by now you have heard from Eddy if not I'm sure he is on his way home. Yolanda try not to worry about him, he will be alright once he is home. No matter how he comes back Yolanda just thank God he is home and safe.

I have a feeling I will hear from the War Dept. this week and I'm not looking forward to it because I almost know what they are going to tell me. My hopes have been so high but now the bottom seems to have dropped out of everything. I really don't know what I will do if Jim doesn't come back. I hope my thinking is all wrong and he may come home yet.

Well, I guess this is all for now Yolanda and I know you will be happy with Eddy very soon. Please write to me as I said before I need letters from friends so badly these days.

Love,
Jessie

The families of those who hadn't survived eventually received confirmation that their loved ones had indeed perished.

The last to receive any information was the family of Lawrence Griggs.

There were 50 Boys aboard the five aircraft that were shot down on this mission. 40 of these Boys were from the 829th Squadron. The other ten were from McNulty's 831st crew. (See Appendix A for summary and details of other losses on this mission.)

✪ The Story ✪

As I searched through the archival records of the 485th Bomb Group for mission reports, I came upon several Escape Statements. As I read the faded microfilm records, I found an Escape Statement for Eugene Brittin. In it he told of being shot down, captured and escaping, in brief, unemotional terms. This was on the night of June 9, 1944. The account of Brittin's escape got my attention because I wanted to write a story about the June 9th mission, during which the 485th suffered its highest losses of the entire war. On the faded document I noticed his return date, March 17, 1945. Must be a typo, but I decided to read the document more closely. It wasn't a typo! After escaping, Brittin had been on the run for more than nine months before he made it back to friendly territory! Here was another story for the book, but I also needed to know more about the man. I conjured up images in my mind of Brittin being this big, fearless John Wayne-like character, fighting his way all alone through northern Italy.

In my search for information I contacted other airmen who had known McNulty's crew and even found someone who had known Brittin. The memories people had of Brittin weren't of a tough guy, but rather of a small, likable gentleman, on the quiet side. For me, it didn't seem to fit, but I had to know more. No one had heard this story, including Lt. Colonel Dan Sjodin, the squadron commander. They must have sent him home immediately after his return. Since I wanted to include a story about the

June 9th mission, I decided to focus on McNulty's crew and tell their story.

I was pleasantly surprised when I located Brittin. I wrote him a letter, explained I was writing a book and told him I'd like to interview him. A week later I received a very polite letter from him, acknowledging he was the person I had been looking for, but telling me the experience was still too painful to discuss. He wrote that he would take the story to his death and asked me not to contact him again. I felt horrible to have disturbed him and honored his request.

After more searching, I eventually located Yolanda Lubanovich Stahl, Ed Lubanovich's widow. She brought the entire crew to life for me, having known all of the men, or boys as she called them, except for Lindsey. She cooked weekly dinners for the crew and still became emotional when providing details of what she knew about some of their deaths. During a series of phone conversations, she told me of her first meeting with Ed, their courtship and marriage, and of that telegram she received, that damned telegram that changed everything. We also discussed those agonizing days while he was MIA, before confirmation came of his POW status. Yolanda didn't share details of his homecoming until much later.

I asked Yolanda to tell me more about Brittin. She described him as a gentle person, very polite and just a nice guy. I told her of my contact with him and it didn't surprise her, because she had phoned him a few years back. They had a nice conversation and he seemed happy to hear from her, but acknowledged it was painful to discuss his own experience. She told me not to feel bad and encouraged me to tell the story of the crew. Yolanda also sent me photos. Now I had faces to put with the names and stories.

I wanted to tell a story that did justice to this crew and honored the others lost that day in June. By this time I felt I almost knew them. I made several inquiries in Italy, trying to locate witnesses who saw the plane go down. A European police friend even used his contacts in Italy to try to find someone who would help, to no avail. I finally made one last attempt, writing to a researcher who had helped people in the past. He did not respond.

Then I was contacted by an Italian, Fabio Stergulc. The other researcher was too busy to help, but told Fabio of my quest and Fabio offered his assistance. Fabio is an entomologist by day and does WWII research as a hobby. My expectations weren't high but Fabio shared my enthusiasm. He amazed me by locating several witnesses, including members of two families who had hidden Brittin! He kept sending more information, even identifying the German pilot who shot down McNulty's plane. He provided medical records from the hospital where Lawrence Griggs died. In essence, he located every bit of information possible and is really a part of the story now. He's a first class researcher and I'm happy the story gods sent him my way.

One extremely important piece of information Fabio uncovered was that most of the D'Olivo family evaded capture when the SS troops came to their home and burned it. They all survived the war and went on to live long lives. In Brittin's report, he indicated that other POWs staying at the house were captured but, according to the D'Olivo's, they also escaped. Brittin's report seemed to indicate he believed most of the family was taken away by the Germans and we now knew this wasn't the case.

Yolanda and I discussed this new information and what to do with it. I had two separate lines of thought. I felt it might give Brittin some comfort to know that most of those in and around the house, like himself, managed to escape. I thought this might be part of what troubled him, the belief that the family and those other men had been taken by the SS. On the other hand, I certainly didn't want to continue bringing up bad memories for a man who had endured so much. Yolanda believed firmly that he should have this information. After several more discussions, Yolanda and I agreed that she would call him and provide him with this new information. She phoned him and he now knows what happened to the family. I hope it gives him some peace. He deserves it. The D'Olivo sisters, whose family risked their lives for Brittin, are happy to know he survived. I am too, and I am also glad we have people in the world like him, people who don't quit in the face of adversity. Oh, I'm also happy that Ed asked Yolanda to dance.

JW

NOTES AND REFERENCES

[1] Most of the crew background came from Yolanda Lubanovich Stahl, obtained in a phone interview on 2/13/04. The states of residence were confirmed through a document sent to Yolanda by the War Department, which contained names and addresses of the next of kin of all the men on the crew.

[2] The history of Griggs and Sheridan was obtained in a phone interview with Murray Sheridan on 11/3/03.

[3] Details of the courtship between Yolanda and Ed Lubanovich were obtained in a phone interview with Yolando Lubanovich Stahl on 5/3/04.

[4] Sheridan suffered serious flak wounds in the back and left arm on 5/22/44 when the aircraft took a direct hit approximately 2' in front of the tail turret, while attacking the Valmontone, Italy marshaling yard. Damage destroyed the hydraulics and the damaged aircraft landed at Bari. Sheridan was returned to the U.S. where he underwent a long recuperation. From phone interview with Murray Sheridan on 11/3/03.

[5] Lt. Colonel Bill Herblin, interviewed on 10/8/04, recalled leading the mission and the fact that one of the other groups had difficulty assembling. Without fighter escort, they were attacked by enemy fighters and lost 5 aircraft that day.

[6] Details of the mission are from Brittin's Escape Statement, dated 3/19/45, and are also a letter from Jessie McNulty to Yolanda Lubanovich, dated 6/2/45. The letter from Jessie McNulty references information obtained from Brittin's parents concerning what occurred on the flight.

[7] The mystery remains as to why the landing gear was dropped. This act was considered a sign of surrender but, in this case, it's possible it was a mechanical malfunction.

[8] 485th Bomb Group Debriefing Statement from T. Sgt. Joe W. South, 831st Bomb Squadron, dated 6/10/44.

[9] 485th Bomb Group Debriefing Statement from S. Sgt. Raymond J. Heskes, 831st Bomb Squadron, dated 6/10/44.

[10] Italian researcher Fabio Stergulc contacted noted Italian WWII air historian Ferdinando D'Amico. Both concur that Scheer, in all probability, was the pilot who shot down McNulty's aircraft. The other possibilities are Italian pilot Chiussi and German pilot Herrmann, but these are less likely. This information was provided to the author by Stergulc.

[11] The observations by the Italian witnesses to the crash were provided to the author in an investigation report by Stergulc, dated 3/11/05.

[12] Date of death confirmed by death certificate from Portogruaro hospital. Stergulc spoke with hospital administrator Gianna Daneluzzi, who found that Griggs' clinical record was missing.

[13] Details of Brittin's's capture, escape, and eventual return to Italy are from his Escape Statement.

[14] Information on the D'Olivo and Nicodemo families and details of arrest and survival were provided to the author by Italian researcher Fabio Stergulc in an investigation report, dated 2/28/05.

[15]Background info on Presotta and Basei was provided by Italian researcher Fabio Stergulc in an investigation report, dated 2/28/05.

[16] Information of Lubanovich's release and homecoming are from a phone interview with Yolanda Lubanovich Stahl on 5/13/04.

[17]Yolanda Lubanovich Stahl collection.

Prisoners of the Bulgarians

In late October of 1944, the Americans were engaged in the retaking of the Philippines. The Russians had pushed into Yugoslavia, capturing Belgrade, and American forces had smashed the Siegfried Line north of Aachen, Germany. On October 29th Major Walter Smith, recently released from the hospital, took off on a little known special mission, its results kept secret for years.[1]

Earlier in the year, Smith, a B-24 bomber pilot, was sent to the 485th Bomb Group from the 55th Wing headquarters in order to gain combat experience. He was assigned to the 829th Bomb Squadron. Smith flew a few missions, but his last mission did not end well for him and the crew with which he was flying that day.

On Friday June 23, 1944, the Boys of the 485th prepared for the group's fourth mission to Romania. For most of 1st Lt. Bob Bobier's 829th Squadron crew, it was their 22nd mission overall and their third to Romania. They were one of the original crews in the group that had flown overseas when the group was initially formed. Today would be different for them. The regular copilot on the crew, Mel Matthews, was being replaced by Major Walter Smith and Bobier would fly as copilot.

Bobier lost one member of the original crew before they even started flying combat missions. When his crew flew overseas, nose gunner Sgt. Leonard Lesch was replaced by a key ground crewman and went overseas by ship. Lesch was killed when his ship, the *Paul Hamilton*, was sunk by German aircraft. Lesch was replaced by Sgt. Harold Jones. He had come by ship to Italy and the remainder of Jones' original crew died when their plane crashed into a mountain enroute to Italy.

2nd Lt. John Hannum was the navigator and 2nd Lt. Dick Doyle was the bombardier. S/Sgt. Christopher Sideratos was the flight engineer/top turret gunner. The ball gunner was S/Sgt. Charles

18. Lt. Bob Bobier crew photo, 829th B.S. Back row, left to right: Leonard Lesh, nose gunner; T/Sgt. Lurker, crew chief (non-flying); Sgt. MacDowl, asst. crew chief (non-flying); George Chesterton, radio operator; Ben Karoly, waist gunner; Christopher Sideratos, flight engineer/top turret; Charles Palmer, ball gunner, and Charles Dameron, tail gunner. Front row, left to right: Mel Matthews, copilot; Dick Doyle, bombardier; Bob Bobier, pilot and John Hannum, navigator.

Palmer. The radio opera-
tor/waist gunner was Sgt.
George Chesterton and at
the other waist gun was Sgt.
Bennett Karoly. Back in the
tail was Sgt. Charles "Red"
Dameron. These men had all
trained together in the
States.

19. Harold Jones, replacement nose
gunner on Bobier's crew

At briefing, the crew
learned today's target was
the oil storage tanks at
Giurgiu, on the banks of the
Danube, which formed the
southern border of Roma-
nia, separating it from Bulgaria. At least they weren't returning
to the Ploesti oil fields with its hundreds of flak guns and hordes
of hostile fighters. It was still a long mission over enemy territory.
They would be flying in the #4 position, the slot, directly behind
and below the formation leader and would be in a position to
take over should the leader encounter problems.

The mission started out uneventful for the crew as they took
off and formed up with their squadron, then with their group, for
the long trip to Romania. The first sign of trouble was when the
waist gunners reported the #1 engine, the outboard engine on
the left wing, was leaking oil. Smith and Bobier looked out and
saw oil coming from the front of the engine, not a good sign. The
oil pressure was still in the normal range so they decided to carry
on, knowing that if the oil pressure dropped too low the engine
would have to be feathered.[2]

The next sign of a problem was when they tried to transfer
fuel from the wing tip tanks to the main tanks. The fuel transfer
pump, located in the bomb bay section of the aircraft, had a bad
gasoline leak and fumes filled the back of the plane. To minimize

the danger, all unnecessary electric and radio equipment were turned off and the remainder of the fuel was transferred.

As they flew on toward the target, the #2 engine turbo supercharger began surging. Although doing little damage to the engine, it caused the engine to vibrate and made the aircraft more difficult to fly.

A while later Bobier noticed the #1 engine oil pressure had dropped from 85 pounds to 50 pounds. This was an indication that most of the oil had leaked out and the prop had to be feathered. The pilots applied more power to the other three engines in an effort to keep up with the formation. They were still climbing and were 4,000 feet below the planned bombing altitude of 23,000 feet. The old bomber just couldn't keep up and they began falling farther and farther behind. Finally realizing they couldn't keep up with the formation, they decided to find a target of opportunity where they could drop their four 1,000 lb. bombs.

They were over Bulgaria when they dropped out of formation. The territory was not new to them and Doyle suggested they head north, crossing the Danube into Romania. They were briefed not to drop their bombs in Bulgaria. Shortly after crossing the Danube, Doyle spotted a factory and military trucks at the small town of Turnu Magurele. Doyle dropped the bombs right on target. Now losing altitude at the rate of about 100 feet per minute, they were lower than 17,000 feet and could easily see the target they had just hit. They turned and headed back toward Italy.

Smith and the crew were all alone and had a long trip back to safe territory. About a half hour later Dameron, in the tail, reported a fighter at 5 o'clock high, saying it looked like an ME 109. There were some tense moments until one of the waist gunners said it looked more like a P-51. The plane passed beneath and then climbed high in front of them, still at a distance that made positive identification impossible. Doyle got a glimpse of the plane and it was shiny silver, unlike most of the German

Messershmitts he had seen on earlier missions. He directed the gunners not to fire until a positive identification was made. Within seconds the gunners confirmed it was a P-51. Bobier went to Channel B on the radio and contacted the fighter pilot who advised them he would provide top cover, 3,000 feet above and behind them.[3] Things were looking up now.

There was a lot of cloud cover beneath them and things were going quite well, until two bursts of flak exploded directly below their right wing, violently rocking the plane and causing the wing to rise vertically. About the same time Hannum reported over the intercom that they were over Sofia! This was not a good place to be, with all of it's anti-aircraft guns.

The pilots took immediate action to right the aircraft and Smith began a series of evasive actions, swinging the big aircraft first in one direction then back in the other direction. There were no more hits, but the damage had been done. They were at about 12,000 feet when they were hit. The plane was full of holes, but no one was injured. Their fighter escort left them.

Suddenly, more bad news. Gunners reported both engines on the right side of the plane, #3 and #4 were throwing oil. It wouldn't be too long before they would have to feather both engines. Since the plane couldn't fly indefinitely on one engine, the situation was critical. As they sank beneath 9,000 feet the #4 engine oil pressure dropped rapidly, so Bobier feathered the engine. Now they were down to two engines. With a few hundred miles to go and mountains to climb over it didn't take a genius to do the math. It was now just a matter of how far they'd make it before they had to bail out.

Bobier hoped they could make it to Partisan territory in Yugoslavia and it appeared they had indeed crossed the border. As they sank to 5,000 feet in altitude, the #3 engine oil pressure dropped. With only one engine left, Bobier feathered the engine and gave the order to bail out, following up with the bail-out bell.

The pilots put the plane on automatic pilot as the rest of the crew began to leave the ship.

Dameron was the first to bail out through the camera hatch in the waist, followed by Chesterton. As Karoly knelt by the camera hatch, Palmer pushed him out and jumped himself.[4]

The bomb bay doors were open as Bobier got out of his seat. He looked back and saw his parachute was not behind the seat where he had left it. He quickly found a spare that had been left over the bomb bay and snapped it on to his harness. He grabbed his maps of the area and then went back to the bomb bay. He was surprised to see Sideratos and Hannum. Both hesitated at the bomb bay entrance. Bobier pushed them both out of the plane, looked back and saw Smith leaving his seat, then jumped himself. In just a few seconds Smith also jumped through the open bomb bay doors.

Up in front, the bail-out bell was clanging in Doyle's ears. Jones backed out of the nose turret and knelt by the nose wheel opening. Doyle had already pulled the emergency release lever to open the nose wheel doors. Doyle shoved Jones and he fell through the opening. Doyle was last out as the plane dipped its wing for its final plunge to earth.[5]

After they had all jumped, the bomber made a diving circle, finally crashing into the side of a mountain about 200 feet from where Palmer had landed. They had bailed out near the village of Tetovo, in Yugoslavia, close to the Albanian border. What they didn't know was that the Bulgarian army had invaded and occupied this part of Yugoslavia. Since the Bulgarians were allies of the Germans, this was now unfriendly territory.

Dameron, Jones, Hannum, Sideratos and Chesterton were captured almost immediately. Karoly felt like he was floating as he descended in his parachute.[6] He hit the ground hard, first on his seat and then hit his head, knocking himself out. When he regained consciousness he buried his parachute. There were sheepherders in the area. As Karoly pondered what his next step was to be, a German corporal approached, armed with a Mauser rifle. The soldier was polite but the message was clear. Karoly was marched the mile or so to a garrison at Tetovo. There he was searched and turned over to Bulgarian soldiers and put in a small stable, where he joined other members of his crew.

Palmer landed safely and immediately hid his parachute. He saw a man herding cattle nearby and approached him. Through sign language and various words he was able to learn he was in Yugoslavia and there were Germans around. Palmer left and began running downhill, searching for a hiding place. He crossed a road and hid in a wheat field after hearing rifle shots. After hiding for a short while he decided to make it to some trees nearby, so he could hide his flying clothes. As he walked across the field he saw a German spotter plane above him, then saw two men about 200 yards away.

Palmer started running back up the hill in the direction of some trees. The men began shooting at him and he hit the ground when he heard the shots, then was up and running again. As he approached the tree line, another group of men came from the direction of the trees and he realized there was no escape. He stopped and raised his hands. Both men who had been shooting at him were civilians. One began making motions to him, but he didn't understand. He threw down his pistol, thinking this is what they wanted. This seemed only to anger the man, who began yelling and aimed his rifle at Palmer. The second man finally tied Palmer's hands in front of him and they began walking. Any movement Palmer made seemed to upset the armed man, who continued to point the rifle at Palmer's head. As they walked, they were met by some Bulgarian soldiers who searched him and took his personal property.

The Bulgarians marched Palmer a mile or so from where he was captured. Here he was met by German soldiers in a vehicle. An English-speaking German officer began questioning him. He refused to answer and was loaded into the vehicle and taken to

Tetovo. As they approached the garrison at Tetovo he heard the phrase from the German officer, "For you the war is over." Hannum, Jones and Sideratos were already at the garrison when Palmer arrived.

Here they were all stripped and searched. Any personal items previously overlooked were taken. As the Boys were forced to squat against a wall, the German soldiers approached them individually, pointed at them and said, "Amerikanski". When they got to Sideratos, one of them said "Greco" and spit in his face, an obvious insult to his Greek heritage. They were not allowed to talk.

Bobier heard rifle shots from the ground as he descended in his chute. They couldn't be shooting at him, or could they? He landed quickly and softly in a wheat field. He disconnected his chute, looked up and saw an armed soldier about 100 yards away. He noticed a red arm band on the soldier's left arm. Recalling he'd been told back at Venosa the Partisans had red stars on their lapels, he thought this could very well be a Partisan. He walked over to the soldier, who lowered the rifle, pointing it directly at Bobier.

At this point Bobier walked back to where he left his parachute, sat down, took off his electrically heated flying boots and put on his shoes. As he did so he saw several soldiers approaching him, led by a German Luftwaffe officer. Oops! The officer spoke excellent English, with a British accent. The German was polite, asking him if he needed medical attention. Bobier declined and the German said, "For you the war is over." The German directed him to go with the other soldiers and to obey their commands. When Bobier looked more closely at the first soldier he'd seen, he noticed the red arm band had a white circle on it with a black swastika. He was captured by a Bulgarian soldier, not a Partisan. This explained the unfriendly welcome.

After the German officer left, one of the Bulgarian soldiers pointed his bayoneted rifle at Bobier, saying things like "Boom!

Boom! Ploesti". Bobier retreated as the soldier advanced and was saved when one of the other soldiers stopped the angry Bulgarian. As the Bulgarians tried to give Bobier instructions, he had difficulty understanding them and their hand movements. He sat down, thinking this was what they wanted. It wasn't, so he lay down. While Bobier was lying on the ground the Bulgarians removed everything from his pockets, then one with cavalry boots kicked him in his butt. This time he got the point. They wanted him to go with them. They marched him to the garrison at Tetovo where he joined several others from his crew.

Smith hit hard when he landed, knocking himself unconscious. When he came to, he hid his parachute and life jacket and began walking around the area looking for his crew. Within a few minutes a large group of armed Bulgarians surrounded him. They searched him, removed his watch and escape kit, tied his hands behind his back and beat him with their rifle butts. The beating was interrupted by a Bulgarian sergeant and then Smith was carried to the garrison at Tetovo.

By early afternoon, nine of the Boys had arrived at the garrison at Tetovo. They were again searched. They were forced to sit for several hours in the sun and were then taken to a stable behind the garrison. They watched as Bulgarian soldiers went into the stable with shovels and buckets to clean out the manure in two stalls. After this, they were placed in stalls, four or five to a stall. There was one small, barred window on the door. The floor was cement and still smelled of urine and manure.

None of the crew was badly injured, but there were cuts, sprains and pains among them. None appeared to need immediate medical attention. They had been fairly lucky. If the missing Doyle was OK, they had been very lucky. As they began to talk about what just happened, they wondered about their bombardier, Doyle. Jones had seen Doyle standing behind him as he bailed out the nose wheel opening. No one saw Doyle after that, but Jones believed he had gotten out. They discussed what to say during interrogation and all agreed to tell their interrogators the pilot was the missing person and he went down with the plane. This might buy Doyle some time.

Karoly was taken out for questioning by several Bulgarian officers. One German officer watched as the Bulgarians interrogated him. He was asked specific questions about his crew, group and plane, but he gave no information. When he was asked a question he replied, "Bullshit". As Karoly was asked different questions his standard reply became "Bullshit". The Bulgarians had limited knowledge of English and were frustrated when they didn't understand him. Finally, they sent him away.

Smith was questioned by a Bulgarian lieutenant before being placed in the stable. The Bulgarian's English was poor. Smith refused to answer any questions and the interrogation ended. Several others were also questioned. That evening each was given a single piece of dry bread.

The next morning when they awakened, Karoly's face was swollen and nearly unrecognizable. Many of them were bitten by fleas, but Karoly apparently had some sort of allergic reaction. They had not been fed anything substantial.

Bobier was called for questioning. His interrogation was similar to what the others had undergone. He was seated across from a Bulgarian major. He gave only his name, rank and serial number, except for telling the interrogators the tenth man, the pilot, went down with the plane. Later, the nine of them were loaded onto a military truck, along with four Bulgarian guards armed with submachine guns and taken to the town of Skopje, the army headquarters for the region.

They were taken to the third floor of the army headquarters building for a more intense interrogation. Smith was asked routine questions, such as the type of aircraft he was flying, the number of engines and the speed of the plane, the number of men on the crew, the bomb capacity and the top air speed of the plane. He refused to answer any of the questions. His interrogators were a Bulgarian major and a Bulgarian general, asking questions through two English-speaking Bulgarian lieutenants. During the questioning a pistol was left on the table. Smith was reminded that the general could have him shot if he didn't cooperate, but he still refused to answer the questions.

After questioning, Smith was left outside the interrogation room for six hours. Hannum was also kept outside the interrogation room and sat across the lobby from Smith. When Hannum smiled at a passing German officer, the officer slapped Hannum hard across the face. These guys meant business.

Bobier's interrogation was similar to Smith's. He was accused of bombing women and children, berated and called an "Amerikanski gangster". Bobier repeatedly refused to answer questions and was sent back to the hallway to sit on the floor with his fellow officers.

Later, Bobier and Smith were called back together for more interrogation. They were questioned about why the Americans bombed Sofia, what the airmen knew about Bulgaria and their opinion of Communism and Russia. The Bulgarians showed great fear of the Russians. They also asked if Sofia would be bombed again. The two officers refused to answer the questions, but Smith told the Bulgarians Sofia was bombed because it was a military target.

Karoly was one of the first enlisted men to be interrogated. This interrogation was more formal than the one at Tetovo. He refused to answer any of the questions. During the questioning he heard a gunshot outside. When he repeatedly refused to answer their questions, the Bulgarians told him they shot someone. His captors appeared to get frustrated with him and told him he had two hours to cooperate. At the end of that time he would be shot if he didn't answer the questions.

Karoly was taken to a cell. About four hours later he was called in again by his interrogators. He was questioned, but still refused to answer. This time he was told he would not receive food for two days if he didn't answer their questions. He still didn't talk and was taken away. He later determined no one had been shot and this was just a scare tactic.

Palmer's interrogation was similar to Karoly's. He refused to answer, except for his name, rank and serial number. His interrogator, a Bulgarian major, told him he had three hours to think things over and he'd be shot if he didn't cooperate.

When Palmer was again called in for interrogation, the interrogator used a different approach. He was friendlier and tried to persuade Palmer that it was silly not to talk. Palmer refused and was told he wouldn't be fed for two days unless he cooperated. Palmer still refused and was led back to a cell.

Dameron didn't fare as well during the questioning. The major and lieutenant who interrogated him were getting nowhere. The major became incensed and began yelling in Bulgarian. A lieutenant, who acted as interpreter, told Dameron the major was going to have him shot for his lack of cooperation. Dameron still refused to talk and was led to a courtyard where he was forced to stand against a wall. Across the courtyard were four Bulgarian soldiers with rifles, all pointed at him. One can only imagine what went through Dameron's mind as he waited for his executioners to take the action that would end his life. After what must have seemed an eternity, the soldiers began laughing and lowered their rifles. The guards led him back to a cell.[7]

After interrogation, all nine men were put into a filthy cell which measured about twelve feet by twelve feet. This would be their home for more than a week, sleeping on the cold, wet, cement floor. They had no beds and a total of three blankets for all of them. Their first meal consisted of a piece of bread, an uncooked sardine and a piece of cheese. Three days later two straw-filled sacks were brought in. Vermin and lice were in abundance. There was no electricity and no lighting after dark.

Once settled in, each was given a small half-loaf of bread and two bowls of bean soup per day. Their eating utensils were dirty, given to them after the Bulgarian soldiers had used them. They were constantly taunted by their captors and by civilian Bulgarian prisoners who referred to them as "gangsters".

During this time other American airmen were brought in. The Boys were allowed to use an exercise yard for one hour each day. This was the only time out of their cells. The bugs continued to torment them at night and Karoly suffered the worst. His legs were a mass of open, weeping sores. There was no medical treatment.

On June 29th Bobier was allowed to use the stinking outhouse. As he took care of business at the latrine, he heard someone whistling or singing "Listen to the Mockingbird". That was odd. This was a popular song with his crew. Suddenly he realized it was Doyle. Doyle was in solitary confinement in a small, isolated cell in a separate part of the building.

Bobier went back and contacted the commandant, explaining that their other crewman was in solitary confinement. Initially, the commandant didn't believe him, because the crew told the Bulgarians during interrogation that the pilot had been killed in the crash. It didn't appear he was successful convincing the commandant. Bobier joined his crew in their cell, glad that Doyle was alive, sad that he had been captured and mad that the commandant hadn't believed him. Later Doyle was removed from solitary and joined his crew in their cell. Doyle told the crew his story.

Being the last out of the plane and caught by gusty winds, Doyle landed on the opposite side of a ridge from the rest of the crew. He lost his left flying boot in the bail-out and landed on that foot, injuring his heel. Upon landing he gathered up his parachute and buried it. He could hear shots in the valley below and hid in the brush, not wanting to be seen or shot. The hillside was covered with sagebrush-like plants and while in the brush, he put on his regular military boots, which were tied to the parachute harness when he bailed out.

After dark, when he felt he wouldn't be seen, he began walking, still limping from his sore heel. He got his bearings and found a well-worn path which followed the rim of the ridge. He walked throughout the night, occasionally stopping to rest and doze. The next day he saw no one in the area and continued to walk, staying away from the valley. Late in the afternoon he came to a cliff. Hearing noises below the ledge, he looked down and saw a rock quarry. In the quarry he saw a man wearing a black arm band, and a cow. The man had a pitchfork. Doyle recalled hearing at a briefing about Albanian civilians stabbing downed airmen with pitchforks. He knew he was near the Albanian border, so he didn't want to take any chances. He found a hiding place and waited until the man and his cow left. After dark he continued walking.

As he walked in the pitch black night he entered a village before he realized it. He heard voices and suddenly there were two civilian men alongside him. Both appeared to be farmers and had rifles. Hoping they were Partisans he went with them to a scattering of buildings. Doyle couldn't understand what they were saying, but through sign language they seemed to indicate they wanted him to wait for someone important. They took him to a house where he met a man, well-dressed compared to these peasant farmers. He spoke French and was, unfortunately, the enemy. Doyle was quickly turned over to Bulgarian uniformed soldiers. He didn't know it, but he was in the village of Grupchin and was now in the hands of the 8th Boundary Frontier Section of the Bulgarian army.

When Doyle realized he was being turned over to the enemy, he managed to remove the magazine from his .45 and disassemble the slide mechanism, throwing the parts into a stream. Lt. Colonel Peter Zafirov was in charge of the garrison. Zafirov brought in one of his company commanders who spoke some English and they attempted to interrogate Doyle. Doyle wouldn't answer any military questions, but did say he was trying to go to Albania.[8] The soldiers put him in a dirty stable for the remainder of the night. He slept on cow manure.

The next morning he was interrogated again. Once again he refused to give up any military information. The Bulgarians wanted to know where his parachute was. He didn't feel it would do any harm to give up this information which would prove he was an American airman and not a spy, but he honestly couldn't remember where he had buried it. The Bulgarians led him into the hills to find the parachute, one guard on each side and one behind him. They were upset when he couldn't find the exact location. He pointed to various spots that looked like the general area where he had buried the parachute, but he was apparently mistaken. When the Bulgarians didn't find the chute, they began beating Doyle on his shoulders and upper arms with their rifle butts. One guard beat him with a pistol.

This went on all afternoon. He would identify an area, the soldiers would search the area, and then he would be beaten. The soldiers seemed to take delight in beating him. Late in the day they still hadn't located the parachute and they finally gave up and took him back to the dirty stable to spend another long night in the cow manure, under guard.

The next morning Doyle was searched again and put on a train, a small tender with flak cars attached. His arms were tied behind him, his legs were bound and he was put on one of the flak cars. The train left and arrived later that day at Skopje. As the train pulled into the station he noticed a lot of bomb damage. He also observed that the train station had a large Red Cross painted on the roof. The Germans and Bulgarians, knowing the Americans wouldn't intentionally bomb a place marked with a Red Cross, used this to their advantage. It was occupied by the military and was just about the only building in the area that wasn't destroyed or heavily damaged.

Doyle was left on the flak car during the middle of the afternoon, tied securely, but unattended. This was a particularly dangerous time, because American fighters would often strafe targets of opportunity while returning from their bomber escort missions in Romania and Bulgaria. He didn't feel safe and was certainly uncomfortable, still suffering from the beatings of the previous day. He hoped the American fighters would find other targets.

Later in the day his captors returned and took him to a building for interrogation. A German was present during the interrogation and again he refused to provide any military information. Three men were in the room, but one was the primary interrogator. When Doyle refused to talk, he was thrown physically out the door and into the hallway. He still refused to talk. He was taken to a room at one end of the building and put in a small cell, alone. There was an 8-inch by 8-inch window high on the wall near the ceiling, and this opening allowed the only light into the room. The room was claustrophobic and empty. He had lots of time to think and he began to wonder what happened to his crew.

Doyle was only allowed out to use the latrine and not allowed out when anyone else was around. At different times he thought he could hear voices and they sounded like American voices. The latrine was outside, a separate tiny building with a concrete floor. A hole in the floor served as the toilet. He found a small piece of paper. He wrote a note on the paper identifying himself, and placed it on a ledge in the latrine. The Bulgarians must have found it, because he noted it was gone the next time he used the latrine.

When he heard voices outside one day, Doyle began singing. He wanted to let someone know he was alive. Until this moment he had not realized the voices outside were those of his buddies. After Doyle made contact through his singing, Bobier persuaded the commandant to allow him to join the rest of his crew. It was a happy reunion.

On July 2nd they were taken out of their cells early. They weren't fed their usual breakfast, but were each given a loaf of black bread and a small chunk of greasy, smelly meat, similar to salami. The crew was marched to the railroad station, along with about 26 other American airmen POWs. Here they began a 2-day train journey, taking them through Nis, Yugoslavia, on to Sofia, Bulgaria, and then to their final destination, Shumen, Bulgaria.

There were heavily guarded by Bulgarian soldiers armed with submachine guns. There was also an armed guard on top of their car. They were warned that if they even looked out the windows they'd be shot. At one end of the car there was a hole in the floor that served as their latrine. The only time they were allowed to get off the wooden seats was to use the hole at the end of the car. The train car was bug-ridden and Bobier suffered hundreds of bites on his neck. Others endured a similar fate. There was no chance for escape and the journey was miserable.

On the night of July 3rd, the train pulled into the station in Sofia shortly before dusk. Here they switched trains. This train was cleaner and the conditions were better. They traveled through the night and arrived on the afternoon of July 4th at Shumen.

When they got off the train they were put on military trucks and taken to the Shumen garrison. One of the first orders of business was delousing of all POWs. Other POWs, both American and British airmen, were also arriving, to join the 28 Americans who came from Skopje. They were all confined in one room. Conditions were horrible. There was one bucket that served as a toilet for the 85 men who were ultimately confined in this one room.

The men were given sacks filled with straw to serve as mattresses. There were only 25 sacks and, as they soon realized, these were filled with bed bugs. All had bites covering their bodies. They were only allowed out of the room for one hour each day to exercise. Each prisoner received half a small loaf of bread and two bowls of watery soup per day. There weren't enough eating utensils, so they had to share. Karoly became ill with a severe case of diarrhea. Others in the group came down with dysentery, malaria or other illnesses. There was no medical treatment.

Smith complained to the guards and finally a Bulgarian doctor came in to look at those who were most seriously ill. Aside from providing a few aspirins, the doctor did nothing to treat the men. Eventually one of the POWs from another crew, who suffered severe flak wounds, was admitted to a nearby hospital. Several days later a few atabrine tablets and a large supply of aspirins were brought in, but this did little to help their injuries and illnesses.

Several days later the POWs were told they were being moved. They were marched a few miles to a permanent camp on top of a hill south of Shumen. The camp consisted of one large building completely surrounded by a barbed wire fence. The camp would ultimately house 329 POWs, including British, Americans, South Africans, Canadians, Yugoslavians, Dutch and one Greek. 300 were USAAF personnel, including nine Yugoslavian nationals downed while flying with the 376th Bomb Group. Among the Americans were ten airmen who had been captured after the low-level Ploesti raid in August 1943. Some of the POWs were in fairly good health, but many were suffering from flak wounds and burns. Others had open sores.

The camp had originally been a Turkish ammunition dump, but had recently been used by the Bulgarian army for other purposes. It sat at the top of Ilchov Hill. There were about 40 guards, a first sergeant and a commandant.

There were two main rooms in the building and six smaller rooms. About 100 officers were housed in one of the main rooms, 185 enlisted men in the other main room, and 50 officers that shared the six small rooms. More straw sacks were provided, but many of the men were forced to sleep on the bare floor. Others slept on wooden shelf-like bunks along the walls. There weren't enough blankets or utensils to go around, so some of the men shared. Conditions were crowded and there was a severe short-age of water. They were initially given one quart of water per day for washing and drinking. Water was supplied daily by a two-wheeled cart pulled by a mule, with a barrel mounted on it. The cart was brought into the camp enclosure.

The prisoners were locked in the building from noon until 3:30 p.m. and from 6:00 p.m. until 6:00 a.m. During times they weren't allowed outside the building, they urinated in a barrel and defecated in a metal gun case. In the morning the containers were carried down a barbed wire-lined path to an outhouse, where the contents were emptied. Even when allowed outside there wasn't really enough room to exercise. There was no elec-tricity in the building. There were five oil lamps for the entire building, but they were often broken or out of oil.

The usual menu was one small loaf of black bread, two bowls of soup and tea. Major Smith was the ranking American officer and took charge as the commander of the prisoners at the camp. For the most part, the guards left the POWs alone if they fol-lowed the rules.

Once settled in the camp, the Bulgarians paid the American officers an allowance, which most of the officers shared with their enlisted men. With this allowance the POWs could purchase ad-ditional food and supplies. A Bulgarian farmer, with an ox-drawn two-wheeled cart, began coming into the camp. Along with eggs, potatoes, cucumbers, apricots and a few other fruits and vegetables, he had items like toothbrushes, tooth powder and razors for sale.

The boys began to settle into their new home. To pass the time, they played cards made from cigarette boxes, picked the lice out of their clothes, drew maps and discussed the progress of the war. News filtered in that the Russians were advancing and it wouldn't be long before they were at the Bulgarian border.

After the first couple of weeks the food began to improve slightly, as they received marmalade for their breakfast a couple of times per week. In mid-August rumors surfaced that the Russians had started their southern offensive. Then they heard the Romanians were capitulating. Soon they heard Romania had joined the Russians. New Allied airmen, recently shot down, arrived regularly at the camp. They had current information, so hopes began rising when they told of more Allied advances.

The boys were taken out in groups of about 50 and marched into town, where they received Turkish baths from real Turks. Afterward they were allowed to buy sodas and beer before being marched up the hill to the camp again. Something was definitely brewing. About this time a Bulgarian colonel inspected the camp, promising more supplies for the prisoners.

At the end of August, YMCA supplies arrived, including two ukuleles, a phonograph, some records and twenty pairs of bowling shoes. The boys were now getting cheese and marmalade regularly. The POWs received confirmation that Romania had fallen. The rumor was true. This was great news!

The Russians were now knocking at their door. All wondered what their fate would be. Would the Bulgarians turn them over to the Germans? Would they be caught in the middle of a raging battle as the Russians pushed through Bulgaria? Major Smith had several meetings with the Bulgarian colonel in town, the purpose being to arrange for the safe release of all POWs. Smith was allowed to send a telegram to Allied representatives in Ankara, Turkey, advising of the situation at Shumen. The situation had changed from when they first arrived. The camp commandant at that time promised to make things miserable for Smith and the Allied airmen.[9] Now things had changed. There was a different commandant and a new attitude prevailed.

Bulgaria was allied with the Germans, but still considered itself neutral with the Russians. This wouldn't last long though, with the Russians at the Romanian/Bulgarian border.

The prisoners were allowed outside the gate, to bathe in a spring and to play football. Things were looking up. They were still under guard and watched closely, but they were enjoying a few new freedoms. They received official word on September 1st that Russia refused to accept Bulgaria's neutrality and demanded unconditional surrender.

The POWs didn't know it, but help was on the way through diplomatic channels. American diplomats in Ankara, Turkey were conferring with a Bulgarian ambassador there and suggested the POWs at Shumen be evacuated immediately by air. A demand was made of the King of Bulgaria for the immediate release of the POWs, but no answer was forthcoming. The Bulgarian cabinet finally authorized the release through a radio broadcast on September 7th. While negotiations were taking place in Turkey, other things were happening back at Shumen.

There was meat in the soup almost daily. Major Smith went to visit the prison commandant again. Smith wasn't waiting for others to arrange the release of the airmen in the camp and didn't know what was happening in other venues regarding his POWs. On September 8th, Major Smith was flown to Sofia in a German Stork airplane, to meet with Bulgarian officials and arrange for the safe release and return to Allied territory of all Allied POWs in Bulgaria. Smith met with the Chief of Staff and the Chief of Operations of the Bulgarian army. Arrangements were made by telegraph to immediately move the POWs by train out of Bulgaria.

Meanwhile, the camp commandant returned to the camp and made an official announcement that all POWs were free and could venture outside the gate. The POWs decided the first ones outside the gate should be those longest held, survivors of the low-level Ploesti raid. Lt. Darlington, a pilot, and his two one-legged gunners, both having had a leg amputated, were the first out the gate. The airmen ventured outside the gate, but didn't go far. They were told they would be leaving in a few hours.

Palmer walked out with the others. While others were celebrating, he walked off on his own, away from the groups gathering in front of the gate. Alone now on the side of Ilchov hill where he could survey the area below him, he was overwhelmed with the thoughts of his precious freedom. He sat down, thinking of all that had happened, of all they had gone through, and cried. Then he joined the others.

It happened quickly. At 1:45 a.m. on September 9th the POWs were loaded onto trucks and taken to the train station. They boarded a train and began their journey, which would take them through Bulgaria and into Turkey. Major Smith met them the next day, having flown back from Sofia to join the train enroute.

In Istanbul they got off the train and marched to a Turkish army base. They removed their clothing, the same clothing most were wearing when they were shot down, took a clean shower and were given Turkish army uniforms. Those who were ill or injured were put into a hospital. Karoly, due to severe infections from the flea bites, was among those hospitalized.

A couple of days later, after a short ferry ride, they boarded another train for an overnight ride to Aleppo, Syria. Those like Karoly, who had been hospitalized, were put in a Pullman car behind the engine. From Aleppo the freed POWs were taken to an Allied airfield where they boarded C-46 and C-47 transports and were flown to Cairo. All were given medical exams. While the others were flown back to Italy within a few days, Karoly and several others were again hospitalized and flown back to Italy about a week later.

Many of the men required hospitalization for injuries and illnesses. Debriefing statements from the returning airmen revealed the Geneva Convention was frequently violated. The medical care for wounded and sick airmen was virtually non-existent. Only the critically ill received any care whatsoever. At least one POW died from lack of medical care while he was critically ill. Many incidents of brutality and merciless beatings were reported by the returning airmen. Most of these reports of brutality concerned treatment shortly after the airmen were captured and

20. Major Smith and crew, 829th B.S., after return from Bulgaria. Back row, left to right: Charles Palmer, ball gunner; Christopher Sideratos, flight engineer/top turret; Harold Jones, nose gunner; George Chesterton, radio operator/waist gunner, and Charles Dameron, tail gunner. Front row, left to right: Bob Bobier, copilot; Dick Doyle, bombardier; Walter Smith, pilot; John Hannum, navigator, and Mel Matthews (original copilot and not on mission to Bulgaria). (Missing is Ben Karoly, who was still hospitalized.)

before they reached the camp at Shumen, as was the case with Smith and the Boys.

The code name for the return of these POWs to Allied custody was "Operation Freedom". The report for this operation describes the treatment of the POWs as follows:

"In summary, it is reasonable to state that the Allied soldiers falling into Bulgarian hands were somewhat harshly treated, and only the very minimum requirements of the Geneva Conferences as pertains to prisoners of war, were satisfied. Medical attention was often lacking and when given was of a low professional level. The Bulgarian physicians seemed to be poorly trained, were indifferent, and were handicapped by lack of facilities and supplies. The spirit and vitality of these men were probably the principal factors in their resistance to illness, injury, and wounds. No evidence is available to show that the treatment in the hospital was discriminatory, as compared to the care given to Bulgarian civilians."[10]

This same report also credited Major Smith with keeping accurate written records of the treatment the POWs received, should the information be needed for an investigation later by the War Crimes Commission. As the POWs were debriefed, stories of horrible beatings and atrocities were revealed by some, while others told of adequate treatment and even acts of kindness afforded by some of their captors. In summary, the treatment of the Americans varied greatly, depending on the location where they were shot down and who captured them.

Based on the reports at these debriefings, General Ira Eaker, commander of the Mediterranean Allied Air Forces (MAAF), directed Brigadier General William E. Hall to go to Bulgaria "to investigate, identify, interrogate and apprehend Bulgarians who had mistreated American POWs while in the custody of the Bulgarian government."[11] Hall took several staff members with him, and eleven former POWs to assist in the identification of those who had committed the most serious offenses. The investigation would be based on the 329 debriefing reports of the recently freed airmen.

Some of the American airmen who received the worst treatment were asked if they would like to return to Bulgaria to assist in identifying their tormentors. Many declined when the other option was to return to the United States immediately. Understandably, many just wanted to go home.

Major Walter Smith was one of those called upon to return. Most of the repatriated POWs returned to their respective bases for a couple of days, and then returned home by boat. Those hospitalized and in need of more intensive medical treatment remained in Italy. Smith was hospitalized on October 3rd, but his next assignment would be to return to Bulgaria.

On October 29, 1944 Major Smith flew to Sofia and joined the investigation already in progress. As Officer in Charge of the Americans in the POW camp at Shumen, he had valuable information with which to assist the investigation. While a prisoner there, he documented many of the incidents reported by arriving POWs and witnessed others. He pled with the camp commandant for medical assistance and supplies and he had lived on one quart of water per day. As the senior released POW, he felt responsibility to identify and apprehend those Bulgarians who had committed the most despicable acts against the Americans. Smith had a personal interest in finding those who had committed these acts against his own crew, including those who had beaten Doyle and put Dameron in front of the firing squad.

General Hall and his contingent found themselves in an unusual, difficult situation. The Russians were definitely in control and pledged their support to the Americans. A group of

21. Walter Smith in Bulgaria.

Bulgarian communists had taken over control of day-to-day functions of the government and placed themselves in key positions. The Bulgarian military, contrary to what one might expect, actively supported the Americans in identifying, locating and apprehending those suspected of committing war crimes against the Americans. Although General Hall met regularly with high-ranking Russian officers, it soon became apparent their support was in voice only. They appeared unwilling or unable to make any decisions at the local level. In late November, the Russians advised General Hall that any American planes flying into Bulgaria needed permission from Moscow. Additionally, the Americans were required to get permission from the Russian commander before traveling anywhere in Bulgaria.

22. Some of General Hall's team in Bulgaria, at a banquet with their allies.

Despite these restrictions placed upon the Americans, ninety-six individuals were identified and investigated for war crimes. Of these, cases against forty were dismissed for insufficient evidence. Eleven were killed in action, missing at the front or died of other causes during the investigation. These other causes included one man shot while escaping, one who was lynched and several suicides. Since the Americans relied solely on the Bulgarian military for information, there were unanswered questions about some of the deaths. Nineteen of those located and interrogated were released, subject to recall. Twenty-five Bulgarians remained in custody when the investigation was concluded in January 1945, awaiting a trial by an American tribunal after a formal armistice was signed. The tribunal never took place.

Lt. Colonel Baldridge, the Operations Officer, concluded in his final memo that no atrocities had taken place while the Americans were in custody of the Bulgarians, but one prisoner had died from lack of medical care. He believed many Bulgarians were unaware of the existence of the Geneva Convention. This, coupled with the bombings of Sofia and what he described as "the fundamental cruelty of the Bulgarian soldiers", led to the poor treatment of the American POWs and to beatings.[12] He also concluded there was a lack of suitable living conditions for the prisoners.

Major Smith participated in many of the interrogations.[13] He was there when Lt. Colonel Peter Zafirov, the commandant from Tetovo, was interrogated about the beating of Lt. Doyle. The commandant denied any involvement or knowledge of the incident and was subsequently released after providing the names of two possible suspects matching the descriptions provided by Doyle. This case presented an additional problem, since Tetovo was in Yugoslavia near the Albanian border. There were still substantial battles to be fought by Tito's Partisans in Yugoslavia, hundreds of miles from where Hall and his group were conducting their investigation in Sofia. This provided one more obstacle. Tito's permission was necessary and the assistance of his

Partisans would likely be needed to locate the suspects. The Hall Mission ended before these men were found.

The garrison commander at Skopje when Smith's crew was interrogated and threatened was placed on the "wanted" list and still hadn't been located when Hall and his staff returned to Italy. Major Smith returned to Italy on January 17, 1945, his assignment completed. Those who participated in the investigation were sworn to secrecy. Many of the released POWs were unaware of the investigation by Hall and his contingent. The results were not declassified until 1961.[14]

(See Appendix B for information on other 485th Bomb Group crews imprisoned in Bulgaria.)

✪ The Story ✪

I knew several crews were shot down in Axis-occupied countries and that some of these countries kept the Americans in their prisons and didn't release them to the Germans. Such was the case when bomber crews were shot down in Bulgaria or Bulgarian-occupied territory until September 1944. This changed when the Bulgarians, with the Russian army knocking at their door, joined the Allied effort. I thought it would be interesting to tell the story of one such crew imprisoned in Bulgaria.

When I began researching this story, I didn't know that Major Walter Smith became the ranking officer in the POW camp or that he was instrumental in arranging the release of all Allied airmen in Bulgaria. Fortunately, several of the crew are still alive and were able to assist me in telling their story.

During my research I was surprised to learn Major Smith returned to Bulgaria, after his release from prison and subsequent hospitalization, as part of the Hall Mission. I hadn't heard of the Hall Mission and was anxious to learn more about it. I was extremely happy to locate one of the participants, Roland Stumpff, and to get his impressions. Stumpff, a B-24 pilot from the 98th

Bomb Group, was shot down one day after Smith's crew. He was brutally beaten by Bulgarian soldiers shortly after his capture. Like Dameron, he was put in front of a firing squad but not shot. When asked, he agreed to return to Bulgaria to identify those who nearly killed him.

I was very fortunate to obtain assistance in Bulgaria from Stanimir Stanev. Stan is a professor at Shumen University. He has done extensive research on the POW camp at Shumen and the American POW issue. Stan is also a retired Bulgarian army colonel. He obtained various records for me and provided valuable input. Our views are different regarding the treatment some of the POWs received, but I am impressed that Stan continued to assist me, despite our backgrounds and differences. I know we've both learned from each other. Stan and I are a bit puzzled about the final disposition of the Bulgarians still in custody when the Hall group returned to Italy. We found no evidence they ever stood trial. They were not held to answer later at the Nuremburg trials, so a few mysteries remain.

While gathering facts and background information, I learned that one of the Boys from the 485th died when his plane crashed. He was buried near the aircraft. Stan was instrumental in obtaining Bulgarian records referencing the crash. The airman's remains were never identified or returned. We hope to solve this mystery for the airman's family. If the answer lies in Bulgaria, I am confident Stan will find it.

JW

NOTES AND REFERENCES

[1] The written investigation, commonly referenced as the Hall Mission Report, wasn't declassified until May 16, 1961.

[2] The description of the mission itself is from Bob Bobier's memoirs entitled *My Final Mission* and from a phone interview with Bobier on 2/26/04.

[3] Doyle believed the pilot was one of the "Red Tails" or Tuskegee Airmen from the 332nd Fighter Group and also recalled the fighter pilot advising he had a coolant problem but would stay with the damaged bomber as long as he could. From 2/7/05 phone interview with Richard Doyle.

[4] Palmer's recollections are from his Shumen diary, maintained while a POW at Shumen camp.

[5] The description of Doyle's bail out and subsequent information about his experience are from a 2/7/05 phone interview with him. The information regarding his interrogation at Tetovo and beating are from his witness statement, dated 9/25/44, 15th Air Force archives.

[6] The description of Karoly's bail out and subsequent information about his experience are from his Escape Statement (debriefing report) dated 9/30/44 and from an interview with him on 12/2/03.

[7] The description of Dameron's treatment at Skopje is from Dameron's account in the *Dameron Family Newsletter,* Spring 1983, Volume 4. Bobier's *My Final Mission* provides additional information about the incident.

[8] From Hall Mission Report, interrogation of Lt. Colonel Peter Traykov Zafirov, dated November 27, 1944.

[9] Much of the information about Smith's capture, living conditions at Shumen and Major Smith's activities at Shumen are from his Escape Statement (debriefing report) dated 9/19/44, 15th Air Force archives

[10] *Operation Freedom* 15-17 September 1944 Fifteenth Air Force Historical Monograph

[11] Baldridge Report directive, 2/1/45 Hall Mission Report, 15th Air Force archives

[12] Memo to Colonel J.H. Whitney dated 2/1/45 Subject: Special Mission to Bulgaria, 15th Air Force archives

[13] The information regarding Major Smith's role was revealed in a 2/25/05 phone interview with Roland Stumpff, one of the original witnesses in the Hall mission.

[14] Palmer and Karoly were both unaware of the Hall Mission and expressed surprise when told by the author.

Munich!

On July 19th, 1944, there was a political shake-up in Japan when Premier Tojo's entire cabinet resigned. The same day an attempt was made on Hitler's life when a bomb planted by some of his staff exploded near him during a meeting. Fate saved him.

Two things happened that influenced Al O'Brien's fate on July 19th. The first was his crew's earlier reassignment from the 830th Squadron to the 829th Squadron. The 829th had suffered horrible losses in its first few weeks in combat, much higher than the rest of the group. Replacements for the losses weren't coming in quickly enough, so O'Brien's crew had been reassigned to the 829th. The second factor sealed his fate. For the first time, he would be flying with another crew. Captain Sandall's top turret gunner was ill and they needed a replacement.

It could have been worse. Captain Sandall was an experienced pilot. His crew was one of the original crews in the group. Sandall was a good pilot and his crew was experienced and respected. Sandall was also a flight leader and occasionally led missions.

When O'Brien went to briefing he saw that Sandall was leading the low box on the second wave over the target. After

23. John Sandall

24. Albert O'Brien

briefing, he collected his gear and headed out to the aircraft with the crew for what would be their final mission.

Their take-off time was 6:45 a.m. and after assembling the group, they joined the other three groups of the 55th Bomb Wing over Spinazzola. They headed out over the Adriatic, and then headed up the Italian coast. There were 36 planes from the 485th that started the mission, but seven returned to base with mechanical problems. Their fighter escorts were right on time and a welcome sight. The 485th recently experienced its share of fighter attacks, resulting in several lost crews and planes.

The trip to Germany was uneventful. The group flew to the east of Munich, made a gradual 180 degree turn to the left and began the bomb run from the north. There was a strong tail wind on the bomb run. As they came over the target, their estimated ground speed was 250 miles per hour, 90 miles per hour faster than their normal cruising speed. The high speed caused the group to miss the target, the BMW factory, but it didn't seem to affect the accuracy of the German anti-aircraft gunners. The group flew through intense, accurate and heavy caliber flak for six minutes.

Just after bombs away, *Yellow G*, Sandall's plane, took a direct flak burst in the left wing. O'Brien felt the impact and had a ring-side seat from his top turret.[1] He saw large holes and realized they weren't going to make it as flames erupted along the wing. He climbed down from the top turret, releasing his seat and disconnecting the oxygen and intercom lines. O'Brien stood at the front entrance to the bomb bay. He saw the bomb bay doors were only partly open, not open wide enough for a safe bail-out. He grabbed the hand crank and cranked the doors open manually. As he did so, the copilot, Lester Knab, bailed out.

O'Brien felt dizzy and light-headed. They were flying at 23,000 feet and he had been without oxygen for a minute or so. He recalled looking back to the cockpit. He saw Captain Sandall getting out of his seat. Suddenly Sandall was thrown back into his seat as the plane went into a spin. O'Brien was thrown into the bomb bay and was being tossed around. He couldn't get out! He lost consciousness.

John Murphy, the tail gunner, managed to get out of the plane. He later wrote to Lester Knab's wife, Ruth:

June 28, 1945

Dear Mrs. Knab:

I arrived home a few days ago and am taking this opportunity to write you all I know concerning the disastrous July 19 mission.

We had just dropped our bombs and were returning from the target when the first burst of flak hit us. On the interphone communication, I heard Captain Sandall ask your husband for a portable oxygen bottle. Evidently, the oxygen system in the forward part of the ship had been shot away. A few seconds later, we were again hit by flak. Captain Sandall called Lt. Knab a second time and said that the supercharger on number two engine was out of order. Up to this time the plane was flying in a normal attitude and everything was quite under control. When a third burst of flak hit us and the plane was badly shaken, I decided to leave my tail turret to investigate. I put on my parachute and started toward the waist. Bourassa, Mueller, and Rucker were preparing to abandon ship. At this point, I saw that the left wing was in flames and I immediately bailed out the left waist window. After tumbling some distance, I was able to straighten out on my back. I could only see one chute in the sky above me. Knowing that only three of the ten escaped, it is my belief that the other seven were in the plane when it exploded.

Lt. Knab was on our original crew in the states and we flew all our combat missions together. For that reason, I feel very close to him, and it is my desire to help you in any way I can.

Please do not hesitate to write me concerning anything I may have omitted.

Sincerely yours,
John J. Murphy[2]

The flight engineer, William Rucker, had similar recollections that he shared in a letter to Mrs. Knab:

June 21, 1945

Dear Mrs. Knab:

Much as I hate to say it, I do not think that there is any hope for your husband if you have not received any news from or about him. I know that this is a very bad way of starting a letter, but I think that you would rather know the exact truth, that is, as far as I know.

To be perfectly frank with you I cannot tell what happened to anyone in the plane except myself. In fact I thought that I was the only one that got out until I ran into Lt. Hale and Sgt. Murphy in a prison camp. We had only a few seconds to get out and everything was so confused. The plane was set on fire just after we were hit and shortly after went into a spin. I only managed to get out at the last moment and I was near a window. The only thing I heard over the interphone was a request from the Captain to your husband, telling him to give him (the Captain) a oxygen bottle-our oxygen system was shot out. Several seconds later the plane went into a spin and the Captain gave the order to bail out.

The officers were in one tent and the enlisted men were in another so we did not see very much of each other. Combat changes some men but your husband remained the same quiet efficient person that he was when he joined the crew. Perhaps Lt. Hale could give you more information about your husband if he has not already written.

I am very sorry that I can tell you so little about hour husband, however if there is anything that I could do or answer any other questions you have, please write me.

Very Truly Yours,
William H. Rucker[3]

Staff Sergeant Albert Slackaway was a gunner in a nearby aircraft. He saw a burst of flak hit the #2 engine of Sandall's plane, tearing off the left wing. Slackaway noted three parachutes come out of the plane before it went into a spin and crashed into a forest.[4] Staff Sergeant Jesse Roberts, in a nearby plane, also saw Sandall's plane get hit in the left wing and saw three parachutes open before the plane crashed.[5]

All witnesses seem to agree that three parachutes opened and three men made it out of the plane safely. What about O'Brien? He must have occasionally asked the same question, for he did survive. After being thrown around violently in the bomb bay,

25. Lester Knab with his wife Ruth.

his next recollection was of floating through the air in his parachute. He had no memory of leaving the plane or opening the parachute.

As he descended, he realized he was coming down in some trees. He hit the tree tops and the canopy of his parachute broke his fall and left him dangling several feet above the ground. He hung there for a while and a German civilian arrived and cut him down. O'Brien felt intense pain in his right ankle. He must have passed out, because the next thing he recalled was lying flat on his back on the ground. The pain in his right ankle was excruciating.

German soldiers quickly arrived and two of them took him to a hospital, a short distance away. On the way to the hospital, he passed his plane which had crashed in some trees. At the hospital his ankle was stitched. He was then taken to another hospital on the edge of Munich. This was a German military hospital, known as a Luftwaffe Lazaratte or Stalag 9C. The hospital was filled with German soldiers. There would be 11 American airmen in his ward. O'Brien was the only enlisted man.

His ankle was operated on soon after he arrived. This would be his home for nearly six months. Major Shriner was the doctor in charge, but the favorite of nearly everyone was the ward nurse, Schwester (Sister) Albana. After surgery O'Brien was able to hobble around on crutches.

The injured Americans ate German hospital food until October, when they received eleven British Red Cross parcels. Near the end of October they received their first American Red Cross parcels, about 78 of them, including a soap package and four medical packages. The Germans gave all the parcels to the Americans to use as they saw fit. They were even given a key to the storage closet where the parcels were kept. They had complete control, which was somewhat unusual for POWs.[6]

With the parcels they began to live like kings. They traded various items for such things as wine, champagne, beer and eggs. At one point the 11 American airmen had eight gallons of beer that they acquired through various trades. The care was excellent, but the real negative aspect, aside from being prisoners, was the bombings by the 15th Air Force. The British bombed by night and the Americans bombed during the day. The worst were the delayed action bombs. They would explode unexpectedly, long after the bombings had occurred. Fellow POW George Brandon recalled there were several near misses, the closest being when the greenhouse at the hospital received a direct hit.

In early December, O'Brien was operated on again, this time to get a bone splinter removed from his ankle. As the holidays approached, the hospital staff made plans for both a Christmas and a New Years party. The Americans were invited to both. The nurses baked cookies for the party. Both parties were very nice affairs. The Germans and Americans shared what they had.

The good life ended for O'Brien and his fellow POWs on January 3rd, 1945, when they were put on a train bound for the main POW processing and interrogation center in Frankfurt. As they passed through Munich, O'Brien witnessed the devastation done to the city by the Allied bombing raids. Along the route to Frankfurt they switched trains. While they were changing trains, a civilian tried to incite a crowd against the Americans, but most of the trip to Frankfurt was without major incident. O'Brien wasn't kept long at the interrogation center. He had already been

25A. Homer Hale   25B. Homer Hale as a POW

a POW for nearly 6 months and didn't have much information of use to his captors, even if he had cooperated.

O'Brien was eventually taken by train to Stalag Luft I, located at Barth, near the Baltic coast. He arrived there on January 16th. There was one frightening incident along the way. The group of POWs was stopped at the train station in Berlin when the air raid sirens sounded. The guards locked the door of their train car and left. O'Brien and his fellow POWs feared they were going to be left in the car when the station was bombed, with no escape possible. Their fears were alleviated a short while later when the guards returned and the train pulled out of the station.

O'Brien eventually had a chance encounter with Lt. Homer Hale at Stalag Luft I. Until this time O'Brien didn't know who had managed to bail out safely. Hale wasn't aware that O'Brien had made it out. Hale told him that two others, Rucker and Murphy, were the only other known survivors.

O'Brien got a job in the mess hall at the POW camp. Rations were very scarce during February and March. In April, thousands of Red Cross parcels were delivered to the camp so there was ample food again.

During the night of April 30th the German guards left the camp. On May 1st, O'Brien and his fellow POWs awakened to find they were no longer prisoners under German control. The ranking officer at the camp, Colonel Zemke, left the camp in search of the Russian forces who were known to be nearby. The Russians soon arrived. The happy Americans tore down the fences surrounding the camp. The Russians supplied food and entertainment for the airmen.

Confusion reigned for the next several days as the American and British airmen waited for word on their evacuation. There was an airfield about three miles from the camp and they were hoping to be evacuated by air, and soon. American officers showed up and told the POWs they were a priority but must be patient.

Within a few days the planes arrived to bring them home. First there was a stop at Camp Lucky Strike, in Le Havre, France. Then O'Brien returned to the U.S. by ship. After two more operations on his ankle he was discharged from the Air Force in November, 1945.

Although not confirmed, it is believed that five of the men were trapped in the plane when it went into the spin. Those crew members who died were Captain John Sandall, 2nd Lt. Lester Knab, 2nd Clement Hurley, T/Sgt. Lionel Bourassa, S/Sgt. Albert C. Mueller and S/Sgt. Jesse Keller. Lt. Knab's parachute never opened and his body was later found in a forest.

 **The Story**

I wanted to tell Al O'Brien's story and the story of the crew he flew with that day. Here was a story of a gunner who had never before flown with another crew. Fate would have it that he would get shot down the one time he flew with another crew. More interesting to me was the treatment he received while hospitalized. It seemed almost unbelievable that he and fellow patients could trade food parcels for beer, wine and champagne. In no way was I trying to show or imply that this was a common POW experience; it simply wasn't. Yet it shows the humanity of a few individuals in this hospital.

When I began writing this story I realized it wouldn't be as complete as I'd like. Few of these type stories are. I had the notes from my interview with Al O'Brien, a copy of Al's diary and some of the background information from the mission. The other survivors of the crew that day are dead. So I started writing the story with what I had.

At the same time I was also working on another story. Regarding this other story, I contacted Dr. Jakob Mayer, a researcher in Austria, and asked for his assistance. We corresponded back and forth. He told me of an 8th Air Force B-17 he located during an earlier investigation. He had been in touch with George Brandon, one of the pilots. Jakob asked me to phone George and give him his regards.

I phoned George one day and we had an interesting conversation. I explained the reason for my call and told him about my book project. As we talked, he told me about the fighter attack on his plane and his realization they couldn't make it back to England with the damage and wounded aboard. They set course for neutral Switzerland, but were forced to land the plane in the mountains near Innsbruck. This was in July of 1944. He told of his injuries, his capture, and of being taken to a hospital in Munich. He described the wonderful treatment at this hospital and said there were several other wounded American officers in the same hospital.

I told George I was working on a similar story about a crew that was shot down over Munich and said that one of the gunners was also in a hospital in Munich and had received good treatment. The more we talked, the more similar George's experience sounded to the story I was writing. Nah, couldn't be. Munich was a big city. There were lots of hospitals. Besides, George told me there were American officers with him. As George continued to talk, he mentioned there was one gunner from the 15th Air Force, but the others were all officers. I finally had to ask him if he remembered the gunner's name. He said he remembered most of the names of the guys with him and would have to think about it for a minute. I asked if it was Al O'Brien. He said, "Yes, that's him", and asked me how I knew Al.

Once again the "story gods" had smiled upon me. I couldn't believe my good fortune that arose from this chance conversation. There were only ten other American airmen at this hospital with Al and I was talking to one of them! The odds had to be astronomical against this happening. We had a wonderful conversation. George confirmed much of the information I already had and provided more details to help me with the story. After my conversation with George, I wrote Al a letter and told him of my phone call. Sometimes it seems like a very small world.

JW

NOTES AND REFERENCES

[1] O'Brien's recollections were recorded in the diary he maintained while a POW and he provided additional information during an interview with the author on 7/10/03.

[2] From letter written by Murphy to Ruth Knab (Mike Knab Sr. collection).

[3] From letter written by Rucker to Ruth Knab (Mike Knab Sr. collection).

[4] Witness statement, Missing Air Crew Report (MACR) #6915, 15th AF records

[5] Ibid

[6] Some of the details about life at Stalag 9C are from the author's phone interview on 2/2/05 with George Brandon, another POW in the hospital with O'Brien.

Cowboy Boots and Parachutes

Septe mber 10, 1944 was a Sunday. Finnish representatives were busy in Moscow signing an armistice with
the Soviet Union. The U.S. First Army was entering Lux-
embourg. In the Philippines, three groups of Task Force 38 were
attacking Japanese airfields on Mindanao. The Boys at Venosa
were also busy.

Most of the Boys hated Vienna. Images of the Blue Danube,
waltzes, beautiful churches and historic buildings were replaced
by hellish thoughts of flaming bombers, fighter attacks and flak
bursts with bright red centers. One trip there could bring on
nightmares. Vienna was one of the most heavily defended targets in Axis Europe and mission briefings routinely reported
more than five hundred flak guns protecting the city and surrounding areas. The gunners were accurate and deadly, as several previous trips there had proven.

It would be the third mission for 2nd Lt. Art Rasco's 830th
Squadron crew and would be the final mission for *Fifty Missions
from Broadway*, one of the original bombers in the group. It was a
tired bomber, having flown many missions since its arrival with
one of the original crews in the group. Rasco's crew had flown a

26. Lt. Arthur Rasco's crew, 830th B.S. Back row, left to right: Arthur Rasco, pilot; Bob Walcotte, copilot; Joseph Stewart, bombardier and Max Childers, navigator. Front row, left to right: Bloyce Jordan, waist gunner; Ray Buster, nose gunner; Ernie Birch, flight engineer/top turret; Ed Kelly, radio operator/waist gunner; Harold Kempffer, ball gunner, and Ray Lonergan, tail gunner.

new B-24 overseas several weeks previously, but it was taken from them as soon as they arrived in Italy, where it was needed elsewhere. Now they flew whatever plane was available.

The crew was very close and got along well. Unlike many other crews, they called each other by their first names, at least when they were not around the brass. The officers and enlisted men were housed in separate tents, but often visited each other. 2nd Lt. Robert Walcotte was the copilot. 2nd Lt. Max Childers was the navigator and 2nd Lt. Joe Stewart was the bombardier. Tech Sergeant Ernest Birch was the flight engineer/top turret gunner. The radio operator/waist gunner was Corporal Ed Kelly. The other gunners were Corporal Ray Buster in the nose, Corporal Harold "Red" Kempffer in the ball turret, Staff Sergeant Ray Lonergan in the tail and Corporal Bloyce Jordan at the other waist gun.

Rasco, a Texan, wasn't large in stature, but he was easily recognizable around the base by the cowboy boots he constantly wore. He was a good pilot and respected by his crew. There were the usual groans at briefing. The crew hadn't been to Vienna before. Their first two missions had been railroad bridges in northern Italy and no flak was experienced at either target. On the second mission, some of the crew witnessed the P-51 fighter escorts as they went into action and shot down two ME 109 fighters in the area. Today would be different. They would get to know flak on a very personal basis.

The planes took off at 7:00 a.m. According to plan they assembled with the other groups in the 55th Bomb Wing. It was soon time for the Boys to enter their turrets and check their guns, standard routine before entering enemy territory. There were

27. *Fifty Missions from Broadway*

different procedures for each turret. The procedure for the ball turret was the most time-consuming.

The turret was in its retracted position, inside the plane. Using a hand crank, Kempffer maneuvered the turret until its guns were pointing straight down. This brought the turret door into a position where it could be opened. He opened a hydraulic valve which lowered the turret into position beneath the plane and then opened the turret door. Now he stepped inside the turret with one foot, grasping the support mechanism for balance. He put his other foot in the turret, lowering himself by grasping the sides and slid into position. He put his right foot on the right foot rest and put his left foot on the range pedal.

Kempffer reached above him and closed the turret door, making sure the door latches were securely locked. He checked the azimuth power clutch lever and made sure it was engaged, and then flipped the main power switch on the junction box alongside his left knee. Alongside the power switch were the two gun selector switches. He flipped both on and turned on the gun sight switch, which was directly in front of his nose. Kempffer turned the rheostat knob alongside the sight switch to adjust the brightness of the sight. He then reached down, crossed his arms, and grabbed two handles on the floor near his feet. He pulled both handles up, taking the slack out of the cables, then pulled sharply and released them. His guns were now charged and ready to fire.

Along with the process of entering the turret and preparing it for combat there were hoses and various lines to plug in. Beneath Kempffer's seat was a hose connection for his oxygen mask. He plugged it into a regulator. Alongside his right ear was the flow and pressure gauge for monitoring his oxygen supply. His heated flying suit needed to be connected to its electrical unit, also beneath his seat. A rheostat adjusted the amount of heat. He plugged in his helmet earphones and throat microphone at the interphone jacks, making sure the knob was in the interphone position so he could communicate with his crew. He checked to make sure the interphone was working by pressing the transmit button beneath his right toe. When he completed all of these procedures he was ready for combat.[1]

28. Harold Kempffer in full flight gear

The other gunners went through similar procedures as they entered turrets and prepared themselves for penetrating enemy territory. There were a couple of differences for the guy in the ball turret, both related to safety. While the other gunners could wear flak suits, there was no room for this protective gear in the ball. There was also no room for a parachute. The waist gunners could wear their chest packs if they wanted and the other turret gunners could keep them nearby. Even though Kempffer wasn't a large man, 5'5" and 125 pounds, there was still no room for a parachute in the turret with him. For Kempffer it was a more difficult process to get out of the plane and far more time-consuming in an emergency situation. He had to reverse the entry process and this took valuable time. Once out of his turret, he still had to get to the entrance to the bomb bay, where he kept his parachute on the floor alongside the bulkhead and attach it to his harness, before he could leave the plane.

After the gunners were in their turrets or at their stations in the waist, Rasco told the gunners to test-fire their guns. Each gunner fired a few bursts to make sure the guns were functioning properly. The Boys in the other planes were doing the same thing. Soon they were over land and one of the crew reported their fighter escorts were in the area. P-38 Lightnings were seen zooming overhead.

One of the engines was running rough as they struggled to keep in formation high over Austria. Rasco did his best to maintain position in the formation, advancing the power settings on the other engines. This was not a good place to be a straggler. After they passed the Initial Point (IP), flak began bursting all around them. The primary target was completely covered by clouds and the group leader decided to bomb the first alternate target, the Osterreichische Engine Works factory. Rasco struggled to keep up with the formation and Walcotte alerted him they were losing oil pressure in #4 engine. Rasco told Walcotte to feather the engine and increased power in the other three. The group leader, using radar to identify the target, dropped his bombs. The rest followed suit.[2]

Near bursts of flak rocked the planes as they came off the target. Four ME 109s approached the group over the target, but the P-38's drove them off before they could be considered a threat. Flak bursts rocked the ship and #2 engine was hit and suddenly stopped. Now they were in real trouble. They fell back as their group rallied off the target. Rasco tried to join a group behind them, but the bomber couldn't maintain altitude or speed. Several minutes later the flak became lighter and finally trailed behind them, but they were now alone.

Rasco contacted Childers on the intercom and asked for a heading over the lowest mountains in Yugoslavia. The two pilots struggled to keep the airspeed at 120 as they made their way out of Austria. A straggler trailing smoke, at a slow speed, didn't have much chance for survival, especially with the German fighters seen in the area.

Rasco ordered the crew to lighten their load by throwing anything not bolted down overboard. The crew complied. Guns, ammo, the bomb sight and other non-essential equipment were tossed. Kempffer got out of his turret and raised it to lessen wind resistance. They continued their descent, trying to make it to friendly territory.

A P-38 dropped from altitude and came up on their left side. The crew waved and the fighter pilot waved back. It was a beautiful and welcome sight to see their protector flying off their wing. Suddenly, it became quieter as #3 engine stopped. Rasco quickly feathered the engine and told the men over the intercom to put on their parachutes and get ready to bail out. Their fate was sealed. There was no way they'd be going back to Italy on one engine. The gunners scrambled to get to their points of exit, attaching their parachutes along the way. The plane continued its slow descent and soon they were down to 3,000 feet. The bomb bay doors and the rear escape hatch were opened.

Rasco heard #1 engine sputter, then struggle to start again. He hit the bailout bell button, yelling, "Go! Go! Go!" over the intercom. Kelly, in the back of the plane, would be the last to leave that section, alerting Rasco when all the others had left. One by one the crew quickly bailed out from the bomb bay or rear escape hatch. Finally, Rasco was alone. He trimmed the plane for descent and turn, hastily made his way back to the bomb bay, stood on the catwalk for a moment and jumped.

The parachutes of all ten men opened. The jolt of Kempffer's chute opening yanked the helmet from his head. Rasco opened his parachute as he fell through the under cast. The stillness of his descent was broken when *Fifty Missions from Broadway* loomed out of the undercast, headed directly at him. For reasons he never fully understood, Rasco pulled his .45 from his shoulder holster and fired three shots at the bomber as it passed within 100 feet of him. The old bomber turned away, nosed down and crashed into the ground.

The Boys were landing in the countryside, near the town of Bos Novi. Kempffer landed hard between two trees. He lay on the ground, stunned for a short while, then got up. He confirmed he was all in one piece, gathered up his parachute and removed the harness. He had landed on a hill. He hid the chute and harness in nearby brush.

Rasco, while still hanging in his parachute, holstered his gun. He remembered he was wearing his cowboy boots and took the boots off so as not to injure his feet in the landing. He dropped his boots when he was still several feet above the ground, bent his legs and landed, breaking his leg! A group of women immediately surrounded him.

After Kempffer finished hiding his parachute and harness, he heard gunshots in the valley below him and then heard familiar voices yelling, "Come on down here!" It had to be some of his crew. He walked down the hill and ran into some local farmers who took him to a farm house. He joined up with Buster, Childers, Jordan and Lonergan. The Boys wondered what happened to the others. The house was filled with locals who came to see the Americans. The boys were fed bread and hard boiled eggs. It wasn't long before one of the local men proposed a toast. A clear liquid was poured into glasses for the Boys to drink and they drank it, feeling an immediate burning sensation. Another toast was proposed and they drank more of the clear, burning liquid, which they later determined was Rackeya, a local liquor.

While Kempffer and his group were enjoying the hospitality of their new friends, Rasco was being put on the back of an old horse and led by the women down the hillside from where he landed. When they reached a dirt road, two men approached. They spoke briefly to the women and the women left. The men took Rasco to a large house in Bos Novi and carried him inside.

The locals checked him out and realized his leg was broken. They cut his pant leg away and wrapped his leg tightly in cloth, then poured cold water on the bandage.

Rasco dozed off, but awakened when a group of people entered the house. Soon he experienced the same ritual as his crew members who were in the other house. His host handed Rasco a glass, poured some clear liquid into it, poured himself some of the liquid and raised the glass to signal a toast. Rasco drank the liquid and had the same reaction as the other Boys, an immediate burning sensation. More individual toasts were proposed, with each man present having the opportunity to make a toast. Within a short while the pain in his leg subsided. The locals continued putting cold water on the bandage and he was enjoying himself. As Rasco continued with the toasts, Stewart and Walcotte arrived. Stewart had a broken ankle, but Walcotte was in good shape.

Kempffer and his little group made several more toasts and were finally led out of the house and put on a two-wheeled donkey cart. They rode for several hours, finally stopping at a house in the middle of a forest. It was some sort of Partisan headquarters.

After dark, an ancient, coal-burning stake-bed truck arrived. The five Boys were loaded into the back of the truck with two Partisan soldiers. The truck took off into the night.

By now Rasco had been joined by Birch, who was not in good shape. It was later determined he had broken his back. Rasco and his contingent set out into the darkness in an old, coal-burning truck. They stopped at a grassy field. By then, Kempffer and his group had also arrived. Nine of the crew were now together and the only one missing was Kelly.

As the men waited in the field, aircraft engines were heard overhead and signal flares were lit on the ground. A C-47 came into view and made a quick landing in the grassy field. The plane's crew quickly unloaded supplies and Rasco and the Boys boarded the aircraft. Another downed American crew from a different bomb group and several wounded Partisan soldiers also boarded. The engines were kept running during the process and the wheels were rolling as the last man boarded. Quickly they were in the air and headed back to Italy.

The plane landed at Bari and Rasco's crew was taken to the Army hospital. They had to fill out various forms and then went to bed. The next day the uninjured were taken by truck back to Venosa. Birch was sent home to the U.S. and Stewart and Rasco returned to Venosa about a week later.

But what of the last crew member, Ed Kelly? Kelly returned a few weeks later, describing a wonderful experience. He told Kempffer he had broken his dental bridge when he landed in a tree, but was otherwise uninjured. He was rescued by a man who had lived for several years in Philadelphia, Kelly's home. He dodged the Germans for about three weeks and finally made it back safely.

✪ The Story ✪

I wanted to tell a story of an evasion that went smoothly. As I searched through files and records I found an Escape Statement for Art Rasco's crew. It was dated September 11, 1944, one day after the crew returned. It certainly appeared routine to me. Here's what it said:

While flying on a mission over Vienna source's plane was hit by flak knocking out No. 4 engine, shortly after No. 2 engine cut out for no apparent reason. Source was unable to keep up with own formation but tacked on to another; however the plane began losing altitude and was picked up by escorting fighters. Number 3 engine cut out so the pilot gave orders to bail out. All crew members left ship successfully and landed near Partisan headquarters, being picked up almost immediately. They were fed and kept at this place until evening when they were moved by truck to evacuation airport and flown out the same night.[3]

Short and sweet, it was just the sort of story I was looking for. During my initial interview with Harold "Red" Kempffer and his wife at their home in Minnesota during the summer of 2003, I realized just how ridiculous it had been for me to even imagine any bail out could have gone smoothly! What was I thinking? I felt like a fool. After all, the story is about a bomber crew bailing out of a stricken bomber over enemy territory. They had never bailed out before and they jumped into rough terrain, with Germans known to be in the area.

My conversation with the Kempffers and subsequent phone calls with Art Rasco confirmed my belief that things really hadn't gone smoothly and it was far from routine. At least three of the crew had broken bones, including one with a broken back.

Still, they were fortunate to get out when they did. The Germans maintained a strong presence in the region. The term "evacuation airport" in the Escape Statement made me chuckle. If the seasonal rains had come, preventing the rescue plane from landing and taking off on the grass field, their return to Italy could have been delayed several months and forced them to walk through the mountains to get back to the coast. They could also have been caught in pitched battles between the Partisans and Chetniks, Partisans and Ustashe or Partisans and Germans. Indeed, they were lucky to get out when they did.

Incidentally, this crew, except for Birch, continued flying combat missions. On six of their first nine missions they didn't make it back to their home base, due to battle damage or other causes. On one occasion they met again their Partisan allies when forced to make an emergency landing on the island of Vis.

In a recent phone conversation I asked Harold Kempffer if Art Rasco ever wore those cowboy boots again. Harold said Art was wearing them as soon as his leg had healed enough to limp around the base. Perhaps, "Once a Texan...................".

NOTES AND REFERENCES

[1] The description of entering the turret is from a phone interview with Harold Kempffer in June 2005. The accounts of the other activities in the back of the plane and of Harold's subsequent actions are from an interview with him on 6/1/03 at his home in Minnesota and from his memoirs *As I Remember*.

[2] The description of what occurred in the cockpit and details of Art Rasco's actions on this mission are from a phone interview with Rasco in October 2003 and from his memoirs *Fifty Missions from Broadway*.

[3] Escape Statement for Arthur Rasco crew, 485th Bomb Group records.

Down Over Auschwitz

T he Cincinnati Reds and the Chicago Cubs played a double header that day at Wrigley Field, each team winning a game. At Sportsmans Park, the St. Louis Cardinals and Pittsburgh Pirates also played a double header, the Pirates winning both games. The Boys at Venosa weren't playing baseball. They were playing for much higher stakes.

The survivors don't recall any feelings of foreboding about the mission they were flying on this Wednesday, the 13th of September, 1944. Most of the crew had never flown together, but all had previous combat experience. When they gathered for briefing they learned from the mission leader, Lt. Colonel Bill Herblin, the target was Oswiecim, Poland. Americans would later come to know it as Auschwitz. The specific target was the synthetic oil and rubber factory. Intelligence indicated there shouldn't be much flak or fighter opposition. Herblin pointed out a large labor camp near the refinery. He cautioned the bombardiers to avoid bombing the camp.[1] There was a collective sigh of relief at the end of briefing. This would be one of the longest missions the Boys of the 485th had flown, but it should be an easy one, a milk run.

This was the first trip for the 485th to Oswiecim, although the target had been bombed by B-17s from the 15th Air Force on August 17th. The Boys had no idea of the atrocities taking place at the infamous concentration camps nearby. If the 15th Air Force brass knew, they didn't share the information with those doing the bombing.

29. Captain William Lawrence's crew (original crew), 831st B.S., with their assigned plane, *HELL'S ANGEL*. Standing, left to right: Art Nitsche, tail gunner; Joe Lawson, nose gunner; Vernon Christenson, top turret; Richard Garner, radio operator/waist gunner, and Everett MacDonald, flight engineer/waist gunner. Front row, left to right: Homer Disharoon, copilot; William Lawrence, pilot; Arthur Wichmann, navigator and Patsy Campolieta, bombardier. Only Christensen, Nitsche and MacDonald were flying with Lawrence on September 13, 1944.

It was the 50th mission for some of the Boys on one crew. Captain Bill Lawrence, the pilot, was completing his missions today and would soon be going home, if all went well. Lawrence often led the group on previous missions. He was considered one of the finest pilots in the group by the 831st Squadron Commander, Lt. Colonel Dan Sjodin.[2] Sjodin often flew with Lawrence and his crew. When Sjodin wasn't scheduled to fly, Lawrence often led the squadron. On this day Lawrence would be flying in the deputy lead position, slightly behind and on the right wing of Lt. Colonel Herblin.

Lawrence didn't look the part of a dashing pilot. At 5'8", he was not a large man. One of his officer buddies commented that even in his dress uniform he didn't look like a pilot, and looked out of place in uniform. He looked much more comfortable playing the organ in the newly-constructed chapel or playing the piano at the Officer's Club.[3] One of his crew, Tech Sgt. Vernon Christensen, recalled how calm and steady Lawrence was at the controls of the B-24, especially in combat situations. He had the ability to fly extremely tight formations, easing into position with no jerky movements. This skill made him a good formation leader, because his smooth movements made it easier for other pilots to follow him in the tight formations. Although Lawrence always looked calm, Christensen knew better, having watched him on many occasions as the plane left enemy territory, descending from altitude. Despite sub-zero temperatures, when Lawrence removed his oxygen mask, he was sweating profusely and the entire front of his clothing would be drenched with perspiration.

Lawrence was 25 years old and single. He was from Little Rock, Arkansas where he had attended nearby Ouachita University. He might just make it home for his 26th birthday, on October 20th. Some of his crew had already finished their missions, having flown with other crews when the group was short-handed due to heavy losses. Today Lawrence would fly with three of the Boys from his original crew. The others were experienced airmen from other crews.

1st Lt. Matt Hall was the copilot and had developed a reputation as an excellent pilot. Matt started out with Lt. Wiggins' crew, another of the original crews, back in May. Wiggins' crew was decimated on June 28th, when they were savagely and repeatedly attacked by fighters while returning from a mission to Bucharest, Romania. Their plane was unable to keep up with the formation and most of the crew were wounded. Despite being seriously wounded himself, Hall and the injured Wiggins brought the aircraft back to Italy. Meanwhile, the gunners were credited with destroying seven German fighters. The plane had more than 500 holes in it when it landed at Bari and was later scrapped. Hall and most of the crew were hospitalized with injuries from the fighter attacks. The entire crew received Silver Stars for heroism.[4]

30. Matt Hall

After this incident, Wiggins' crew was broken up. Those able to return to duty were assigned to various other crews. Hall was eventually assigned to be Lawrence's copilot, after the original copilot became 1st pilot on another crew. This would be Hall's 37th mission. He was anxious to finish his 50 missions and return home to his new wife. His 21st birthday was in November and he wanted to be home to celebrate.

The bombardier was 2nd Lt. Frank Pratt. Pratt was also one of the originals in the 485th. He was from Ted Jacobs' crew. His crew finished their missions and they were on their way home. This would be Pratt's 47th mission. He had been flying almost daily, filling in on various crews that needed a bombardier. At 28 years old, he was an old timer among the flying personnel. Pratt fell behind on his missions when he had minor surgery at Bari.[5]

31. Frank Pratt

The plane in the deputy lead position would take over as group leader should anything happen to the mission leader. For this reason, today the crew had three navigators including a radar navigator, instead of the plane's normal compliment of just one. The first navigator was 2nd Lt. Dan Blodgett. Blodgett was from Eddie Neitzel's crew and had already flown 36 missions. A recent bout of dysentery caused him to miss a few missions with his crew. He wanted to finish his missions and return home with his own crew, so he was trying to catch up and had volunteered for this mission. This was his first time in combat with another crew. Blodgett knew he was in good company, but the 21 year-old was still relieved this was going to be a milk run.[6] Today they were flying in a radar-equipped plane. Blodgett's station was at a desk behind the pilot, where he would plot the course with the assistance of the other two navigators.

1st Lt. George Winter was the second navigator. Winter was flying his 50th mission and was another original in the group, from Ed Stauverman's crew. In a lead or deputy lead plane, one of the navigators flew in the nose turret, replacing the regular gunner. This navigator used pilotage, watching different landmarks on the ground from the cramped position in the nose

32. Dan Blodgett

33. George Winter

turret, to plot the course. Blodgett and Winter flipped a coin to decide on their respective positions for the mission. Blodgett won the toss, relegating Winter to the nose turret, where he would also man the twin .50 caliber machineguns in the event of a fighter attack.

The third navigator was 2nd Lt. Irving Paul Canin, the "PFF" or radar navigator, also called the "Mickey Operator". In a radar-equipped lead or deputy lead plane, Canin's position was on a seat, back to back with the copilot, facing the rear of the plane. From this position he monitored his radar scope. Canin was not only from another crew, but also from a different squadron, the 828th. Radar was new to the 485th Bomb Group and there were few radar operators. They were shared among the squadrons, but they always flew in the lead or deputy lead planes and only on radar-equipped aircraft. The 21 year-old from New York was a fairly recent arrival at Venosa and this would be his 4th mission. His parents were Russian immigrants.[7]

34. Paul Canin

35. William Eggers

Tech Sgt. William Eggers came from Missouri. This was his 50th mission. Eggers was from John Jones' crew and was filling in as radio operator. He was known as "Sparks" by the Boys on his regular crew. He was sharp and somewhat reserved, well-liked and respected by his crew. His station on this radar-equipped plane was in the waist. He was single and from St. Louis.[8]

Staff Sgt. Lewis Kaplan flew as a waist gunner on this mission. The ball turret, Kaplan's normal position, was replaced by a radar dome on this plane. "Kap", as the Boys called him, was single and from New Jersey. To his family he was known as Lenny. He shared something in common with the radar operator, Paul Canin. Kaplan's family was also from Russia. He recently turned nineteen, shortly before shipping overseas. His crew arrived in June and was broken up when his pilot was taken off flying status. He filled in as a replacement gunner with other crews. Kaplan, like most boys his age, really enjoyed movies and attended them whenever he got the chance. He had already completed 35 missions in the brief time he had been in Italy.[9]

36. Lewis Kaplan (center) with two of his original crew, Burl Jackson (left) and Emil Manweiler (right). Jackson was later wounded, but finished his 50 missions. Manweiler was killed on his 50th mission on November 5, 1944 in a mid-air collision.

Staff Sgt. Art Nitsche, the tail gunner, was from Lawrence's own crew. He fell a few missions behind the others, having been wounded earlier. Art was outgoing, friendly, likable and at ease with everyone, officers and enlisted men alike. Art was single and from Connecticut.

Tech Sgt. Everett MacDonald was the flight engineer and waist gunner. MacDonald was on his 50th mission. He was from Massachusetts and married. His wife became pregnant just before he went overseas and he was anxious to get home to her. "Mac" was another original from Lawrence's crew. He was older than most of the crew, in his late 20's. A good-looking man, his dark hair had turned white in the 4 months he had been flying combat missions.

Another gunner from Lawrence's own crew was Tech. Sgt. Vernon "Chris" Christensen, the top turret gunner and assistant flight engineer. This was his 50th mission. He was an unmarried, second generation American of Danish ancestry, from rural Montana. Christensen was glad to be finishing his missions and very happy that this would be a milk run.[10]

As the crew gathered around the aircraft in preparation for the mission, some of them met for the first time. The radar-equipped plane was new, a shiny, natural metal finish aircraft. There was good-natured kidding among some of the old hands, particularly among those who were finishing their missions today. Nothing could be better than a milk run to finish their tour. Tomorrow, combat would be a thing of the past.

37. Vernon "Chris" Christensen

As the pilots pre-flighted the plane, Paul Canin suddenly realized he had forgotten the flight information back in the briefing room. This wouldn't do! Yelling to one of the crew that he'd be right back, he jumped to the ground through the open bomb bay doors,

38. 485th Bomb Group radar-equipped plane. Note dome beneath aircraft in place of ball turret.

managed to find a jeep nearby and raced back to the briefing room. He found his portfolio on a chair, grabbed it and raced back to the flight line. His airplane was already taxiing to the runway when he arrived. The bomb bay doors were opened for him as he ran to the airplane and scrambled aboard. It took him a little while to settle his nerves and prepare for the long mission ahead. This one wasn't starting well for him.[11]

The group began taking off at 6:35 a.m. Of the 28 aircraft scheduled for the mission, six would return to base with various malfunctions before reaching the target. The planes formed up with three other groups, the 485th being the third group in line. The formation continued north over the Adriatic. They were eventually joined by their fighter escorts, consisting initially of 30 P-38 twin-engine airplanes. A short while later, 30 P-51 fighters joined the force and were a very welcome sight on this long trek to northern Europe, most of it over enemy territory. No enemy fighters were sighted as the group continued north and the trip to the target was uneventful.[12]

As the group began the bomb run, smoke obscured the target. The Germans were becoming very efficient with their smoke-producing generators. There were also clouds over the target, so the bombardier in the lead aircraft was using the target data supplied by the radar navigator. Canin was also providing distances to the target from his radar scope to Pratt and Winter. Pratt would drop the bombs when he saw the lead plane begin to drop, unless something happened to that aircraft. In that case he would become the lead bombardier and the other planes in the formation would drop their bombs on his lead.

Suddenly anti-aircraft fire was bursting around them. These guys weren't searching for the range; they already had it! Christensen looked down from his turret. The parachute he placed just below him on the flight deck at the beginning of the mission was gone! He yelled into the intercom that someone had taken his chute. A few moments later he saw a hand place a parachute beneath him. It wasn't the same one he put there, but at least he had one. The shells continued bursting around them, rocking the plane violently. Some milk run!

The bomb bay doors were opened. Just before the bombs were dropped, the bomber took a direct flak hit in #3 engine, inboard on the right side of the plane. The engine burst into flames. The bomber fell out of formation and began a slow spiral as the pilots fought to bring the plane under control. Christensen, from his position in the top turret, had a clear view of the flaming engine, just a few feet from him. He could see the aircraft was doomed. Christensen yelled over the intercom, "The engine is on fire! We've gotta get out!" There was no bail-out bell. This part of the electrical system must have been knocked out.[13]

Winter and Pratt, in the nose of the plane, realized they were in serious trouble. Pratt heard the explosion and felt the plane shudder about the same time he released the bombs. He heard someone yell over the intercom that the plane was on fire. Pratt looked out a window on the right side of the plane and saw the wing on fire. The right wing was bending upward and he knew he had to get out. He hit the mechanism to release the nose wheel doors and sat down, dangling his legs outside the plane and prepared to jump.

Meanwhile, Winter had left his position in the nose turret. When he looked back and saw no feet at the rudder controls in the cockpit, Winter realized the pilots had left their positions. He saw Pratt sitting over the nose wheel opening, slapped him on the back of his head and yelled, "Go!" Pratt jumped first, closely followed by Winter.[14]

Canin saw flames lapping into the plane through the open bomb bay doors. He tried dousing the flames with a fire extinguisher, but to no avail. Smoke rapidly engulfed the flight deck.[15]

Christensen felt groggy. His oxygen system must have been malfunctioning as he released his seat and dropped to the flight deck. He picked up the parachute, trying to clip it to his harness. He couldn't get it hooked. He just couldn't get his hands to clip the parachute to the rings on the harness. The lack of oxygen was affecting him. Blodgett saw what was happening and clipped the parachute for Christensen, turned him around and pushed him toward the open bomb bay.

Christensen got down on the catwalk, looked back, and saw both pilots on the flight deck behind him. He couldn't think clearly and hesitated for a moment, trying to get his bearings. Blodgett approached and pushed Christensen out of the plane and into the slipstream, then jumped himself.[16]

Canin was next. He looked back and saw Lawrence and Hall. Both were on the flight deck behind him, waiting for him to leave so they could bail out. As he prepared to jump, the aircraft went into a spin, trapping him and the pilots inside. They couldn't get out! The centrifugal force pinned them inside the plane, plastered to the walls as the bomber went into its death dive. The men in the plane were helpless against this force of nature as the aircraft screamed downward, trailing fire and smoke. Their struggles were hopeless as the three men were thrown against parts of the plane and against one another. The aircraft spun and continued its dive. During one of its violent maneuvers, Canin was hurled out the open bomb bay doors, while Hall and Lawrence remained captives. Canin regained his bearings once clear of the plane and recalling his training, counted to 25 before pulling the ripcord on the parachute. The chute opened with a pop and slowed his descent.

As Canin swung from side to side in his parachute, he became physically ill, the only time he ever experienced air sickness. He looked below him and saw a wooded area. He tried to maneuver his parachute so he would land in the woods, thinking he might hide there until nightfall. When he looked down again, he saw German soldiers on motorcycles following his descent as he drifted over farmland.

As soon as Canin hit the ground the Germans captured him. They took his pistol and an older German soldier, about 50 years old, grabbed his left arm. A younger soldier, who appeared to be 15 or 16, held his right arm. The two soldiers marched him to a nearby truck. The older soldier was shouting at him and making hand gestures, indicating they were going to hang him. Canin looked straight ahead, avoiding eye contact with the angry soldier. He felt the other soldier tugging at his right arm and glanced sideways. The younger soldier was smiling and shaking his head, offering much-needed reassurance to Canin that he was not going to be hanged.

Meanwhile, Blodgett floated down in his parachute. He fell about 1,000 feet before pulling the ripcord. When he got his bearings and looked around, he noticed what a beautiful day it was. As Blodgett descended, he felt the warm air brushing against him, unlike the frigid, below zero temperatures at high altitudes.

He could see another parachute in the distance, at about the same altitude. The bombers were gone and it was now quiet. His own airplane was nowhere in sight. The serenity was broken when Blodgett landed. He heard the words, "Up Hands!" He turned and saw a German soldier pointing a rifle at him, accompanied by a 12 year-old Polish boy.

Christensen doesn't remember pulling his ripcord, but has a clear recollection of hanging from the shroud lines. His helmet had blown off in the wind. His heavy sheepskin flying boots were also gone, most likely a result of the shock from the chute opening. He felt cold and his arms were burned. His first thoughts were of his parents and the impact the telegram would have on them, the one which said "Missing in Action". He felt a sense of disbelief. This was his 50th mission, a milk run. This couldn't be happening to him, but it was!

As Christensen dropped to a lower attitude, he began to feel warmed by the sun. He looked around and saw three parachutes, one below and two above him, all in the distance. He heard the familiar sounds of barnyard animals and could hear the voices of people talking and the sounds of children. He was landing in the country.

The voices brought him back to reality and he thought about his landing as he quickly approached the ground. He landed on his heels against a creek bank. He fell back on his head, the impact knocking him unconscious momentarily. When he came to, he rolled over onto his stomach, and then rose to his hands and knees. He unbuckled his parachute from the harness and started to stand when he saw German soldiers and farmers approach from over the creek bank. One of the soldiers yelled, "Up hands! Up hands!" He complied and the soldier yelled, "Pistolen! Pistolen!" Christensen understood the soldier wanted his pistol. He didn't have one, so he stood there with his arms raised. He felt a coldness descend upon him, unlike the feeling of warmth he felt while floating down. He didn't know it at the time, but this was the prelude to many similar feelings in the coming months. He looked across a field and saw a smoking aircraft engine, another painful reminder of what just happened.

The soldiers all had rifles pointed at him. Christensen reached into one of his pockets and produced a pack of cigarettes. There were two cigarettes left, so he offered one to the soldier who seemed to be in charge and smoked the second himself. Christensen had landed on the outskirts of the Wadowice and the soldiers marched him into town.

Pratt and Winter were the first men out of the plane. Shortly before getting to the I.P., Pratt crawled back to the bomb bay area and used the relief tube, a funnel-shaped device in which the airmen could urinate. This necessitated unbuckling one of the parachute harness leg straps. Pratt forgot to buckle the strap before he bailed out. This meant only one leg was attached to the harness and he was fearful he would fall through the harness. He held firmly to the shrouds as he hung from the parachute. To complicate matters, he heard "whizzing" noises near him, followed by loud reports from the ground. He realized the Germans were shooting at him, but he was helpless to do anything about it.

Pratt landed in a plowed field. Within minutes a motorcycle with a sidecar drove up to him and stopped. A uniformed German soldier was on the cycle. The man in the sidecar, a heavy set older man in civilian clothes, got out and picked up Pratt's parachute. Both motioned for Pratt to get into the sidecar. He got in and the soldier drove him to nearby Wadowice.

Winter looked down from his parachute and realized he was going to land in a cleared field. He knew capture was imminent. He unholstered his .45 caliber pistol and threw it away before landing. Farmers approached after he landed and he gave one of them his parachute. In a few minutes later, German soldiers drove up in a car and took him prisoner. One of the soldiers reclaimed the parachute and Winter was put into the back of a nearby truck and driven to Wadowice.

While the prisoners were being taken to town, other events were taking place in the countryside. The aircraft terminated its death dive in a clearing near a forest, spilling four airmen shortly before it crashed. Two other airmen were found dead in or near the wreckage.[17]

The weather was clear over the community of Zygodowice. Many locals were outside, working the fields or on labor details, supervised by armed German soldiers. This was an occupied country. When the Germans invaded Poland they claimed the border area as their own, declaring it part of the Third Reich. In this region of Poland the Skawa River formed the new border, defended and patrolled by German troops. The people of Zygodowice were on the Polish side of the border. Conditions on this side of the river were much more oppressive and the treatment by the German occupiers was harsh.

The first sign of the impending tragedy was the sound of anti-aircraft fire, miles away at Oswiecim, mixed with the rumbling sounds of bombs exploding in the vicinity of the refinery. Minutes later the high-flying airplanes could be seen, heading east. The group of planes then turned south and flew over Zygodowice.

One bomber was lagging behind the formation, trailing smoke, flying slower and descending. It was obviously in trouble. Several white parachutes popped out of the plane. The people watched as the aircraft made an abrupt turn to the left, and then went into a spin, spiraling towards earth. Accounts differ, but most heard an explosion when the aircraft was still several thousand feet in the air and watched as parts began breaking off the plane. Many described a horrible noise the plane made as it plunged to earth, its engines screaming.

Rudek Bolestaw, a 15 year-old boy, was on the other side of the Skawa, in the Third Reich, when he looked up and saw the smoking bomber, turning in sharp circles. He heard a large explosion as he watched bomber plummet, pieces falling off the plane.[18]

Tadeusz Kowalczyk was standing on a nearby hill when he saw the plane falling. At approximately 1500 feet one of the engines flew off the plane, causing the plane to spin to the left. Several parachutes came out. Kowalczyk was on one of the forced work details. He watched as the German soldiers supervising the work detail grabbed their rifles and began shooting at the airmen in their parachutes. Debris from the aircraft was still falling earthward as the Germans shot upward. Kowalczyk went to the location of the crash and saw five American airmen, all dead, lying on the ground in a straight line, about 50 yards apart. A short while later, a sixth American was found in a nearby field.[19]

39. Stefan Wiktor

Stefan Wiktor was a 16 year-old boy who was also on a work detail. He was digging trenches for communication cables when he heard bombs exploding in the distance and looked up and saw anti-aircraft shells bursting around a large formation of aircraft. The formation flew right through the exploding shells. One of the planes fell out of the formation, smoking. As it descended he saw it was on fire. Wiktor saw parachutes coming from the plane. They seemed to be coming out in pairs. The bomber made a sharp left turn and spiraled downward and Wiktor saw it explode, with pieces falling off. He watched the plane hit the ground, the left wing striking first, about a kilometer from where he was working. When the bomber hit the ground there was another large explosion and fire engulfed the wreckage.

The Germans supervising Wiktor's work detail got in cars and quickly drove to the crash site. Wiktor and some friends ran to the site, arriving a few minutes later. When he got there, he saw two dead flyers on the ground near the plane. The Germans had already stripped the flyers of their clothing. When Wiktor and his friends tried to approach the plane, German soldiers yelled, "Raus! Raus!" Wiktor and his friends left.[20]

Maria Skrzynska lived close to the crash site. She and two other friends saw the falling bomber and watched one airman fall from the plane shortly before the crash. Maria watched the plane explode in the field. She and her friends ran to the airman, but quickly realized he was dead. Within seconds German soldiers arrived. One of the Germans raised his rifle to hit the American flyer, but stopped when he saw the airman was already dead. A crowd of people gathered and the German soldiers chased the civilians away.[21]

Antoni Rams saw the burning plane fly overhead. He saw two airmen, without parachutes, spill from the plane. He went to the closest one. The airman's body was jerking, indicating he was still alive. A German soldier, Sgt. Sikora, arrived and beat the airman in the head with his rifle butt until the airman stopped moving. Sikora then took the flyer's wallet and watch. Rams saw the second airman about 200 yards away. The airman wasn't moving, but Rams didn't see if the German did anything to this flyer because he was ordered to go home.

The bomber crashed in a field that was being plowed. Franciszek Opalinski was plowing his field when the bomber came roaring toward him. Franciszek called to his 22 year-old daughter, Maria, who was working with him. The big bomber crashed right in front of them, exploding and spewing fire from its engines and gas tanks onto the field. He looked for Maria and found her wrapped in flames. In a panic, she had run directly into the flames. She was rolling on the ground, struggling to free herself from her burning clothing. Franciszek got the flames out,

40. Maria Opalinski

but the horse had run away when the bomber crashed. With help from neighbors, he finally got her to the hospital on the other side of the river. Doctors at the hospital said they couldn't save her, so Franiszek took her home. Maria died twelve days later from her burns, just one day before her 23rd birthday.

The bodies of the six dead Boys were gathered together. The Germans stripped them and ordered the local farmers to bury the Boys in a common grave. The Poles dug a grave approximately two meters wide and three meters long. As the flyers were being stripped of their clothing, the Poles begged the Germans to allow the Boys to be buried in their underwear. One soldier commented that there were plenty of people who could use the clothes and refused to honor the request.

The Poles carefully lined the bottom of the grave with fir branches, and then placed the Americans in the grave. They placed more fir branches on top of the bodies before covering them with dirt. The Poles were ordered to stay away from the gravesite, but the soldiers permitted them to put a wooden cross on the grave. One of the men in the Kowalczyk family made a wooden cross and inscribed it, both in Polish and German, "Here rests six American flyers 13 September 1944".

After the burial, and unknown to the Germans, locals brought wreaths of fresh flowers and candles to the gravesite. Maria Skrzynska came to the site with her sister Janina, bringing

41. Maria and Janina Skrzynska, the two Polish sisters who were caught by the Germans placing flowers and wreaths on the graves of the Americans.

flowers. As the girls prayed at the site, they were caught by a German patrol. The soldiers belittled them and threatened both with imprisonment at Auschwitz if they returned.[22] The Germans kicked the flowers off the grave, but this didn't deter the girls. They returned later to rearrange the flowers and cared for the gravesite throughout the remainder of the war.

The five survivors were gathered together at some point. Canin recalls being taken to the local police station. Pratt remembers being taken to some sort of an institution where there were women, dressed in black robes and white hats, but doesn't know where it was. It was likely both were describing the same place, the local German headquarters in Wadowice, where the Germans had taken over part of a convent. The five Boys were eventually brought together. Several recall being strip-searched in a gymnasium, in front of civilians, including women.[23]

They tried to piece together what had happened to the other Boys. Why hadn't those in the back of the plane bailed out?

Surely, they must have known the plane was on fire. Were they wounded or already dead? Canin was certain none of the others had gotten out, due to the spin, although none of them actually saw the plane crash. Christensen knew that MacDonald and Nitsche had bailed out once before, during training and knew they weren't afraid to bail out. Deep within himself, Christensen knew he had lost four of his good buddies, along with two other fine airmen. Blodgett voiced his frustration at his bad luck of flying just one time with another crew and getting shot down. Some were nursing cuts, bruises and minor burns. They wished there had been more time to check on the others in the back of the plane. Maybe they could have helped them, but time was the one precious commodity they didn't have.

After the first night in captivity, guards came and led Christensen away. Pratt watched as Christensen left, wondering what was going to happen to him. Pratt noted Christensen's staggering gait, caused by ill-fitting, electrically-heated flying boots.

The officers were taken by train to Frankfurt on Main for interrogation, along with another group of American POWs. Canin was also taken to Frankfurt by train, but separate from the others. Several planes from other bomb groups had gone down that day. Only one other from the 485th was lost. 2nd Lt. Jack Carter's 831st Squadron plane was hit by flak after dropping its bombs, and one engine was feathered. Losing fuel, they headed for the Island of Vis. Realizing they wouldn't make it, Carter ordered his crew to bail out over Yugoslavia. He was fatally injured during the bail-out, but the other members of the crew were picked up by Partisans and made it safely back to Italy.

The officers were separated at Frankfurt and placed in solitary confinement in tiny cells. They later faced interrogation by Nazi officers. Canin had forgotten to wear his dog tags and his interrogator threatened he could be shot as a spy. He was particularly vulnerable for another reason; he was Jewish. His interrogator already had a vast amount of information about him, even knowing where he attended high school. Although the interrogator had this information, Canin refused to cooperate further, giving only his name, rank and serial number.

During one evening session Canin was interrogated by several high-ranking German officers. They knew he was Jewish and insulted him by telling him they were surprised to see him, because Jews usually had others do their fighting. When he refused to react, they began insulting President Roosevelt. When that didn't get the desired reaction, they told him they knew he was a radar officer. The questioning turned to his training and skills. Canin fabricated a story that seemed to satisfy his captors. He was led back to his cell. He had been in solitary confinement for five days. The next day he was allowed to join other airmen. He was put on a train and taken to Wetzlar with POWs. Here, Canin was met by Red Cross representatives, who asked his name and information about his next of kin. He was given clothes, a shower and a Red Cross parcel with toilet articles. The next day he was on another POW train, destination Stalag Luft I at Barth, Germany. All four officers would eventually end up at Barth.

Blodgett, during his interrogation, was surprised at how much the interrogator knew about him and his crew. The interrogator even told him the name of his regular pilot, Neitzel.

Pratt recalled that his interrogator spoke perfect English. In the first session Pratt refused to reveal more than his name, rank and serial number, so he was taken back to his cell. The next day he was taken to the same interrogator. He refused to answer any additional questions. At that point his interrogator told him his squadron (831st), bomb group (485th) and base (Venosa). These Germans were pretty sharp.

Pratt was put on a POW train, destination Stalag Luft 1 at Barth. He was put into a compartment with seven other POWs, one of them a Belgian. The train was slow-moving, heavily guarded and the trip took three days. Pratt saw a handle on the wall of the compartment with a wire attached. Being familiar with trains, he had a hunch he knew the purpose of the handle. Bored, with nothing else to do but ponder his fate, he couldn't resist the temptation. He pulled the handle, causing the train to come to a screeching halt. As the handle dangled, Pratt tried unsuccessfully to push it up into its resting place. Guards rushed into the compartment and caught him red-handed. One guard told him in German he would be shot. The Belgian translated but, even without the translation, Pratt knew he was in serious trouble and had plenty to ponder during the remainder of the journey. On his arrival at the camp, the same guard was still with the POWs. The guard told him he'd be shot in three or four days. Fortunately, that was the last Pratt heard of the incident.

Christensen, after his separation from the officers, was also taken to Frankfurt by train and placed in solitary confinement. In the cell was a bunk covered with a small straw mat. A folded blanket lay on top of the bed. In the corner stood a metal can, his toilet. A small, barred window permitted a little light into the room. Tired and hungry, he tried to sleep. During the night his thoughts turned to the ones who hadn't made it out of the plane. He was the only survivor from his original crew. They had been through so much together and had almost finished their 50 missions safely. They shared so much together; the training, the partying, the family stories, nearly everything but death.[24]

He thought again of his parents and the telegram they should have received by now, informing them he had been shot down. He wondered how they'd react. He also wondered who'd get his personal "stash" in his tent. He had accumulated a lot of gear since the group started flying combat missions. Each time a plane went down, friends from other crews would raid the tents of the downed airmen, taking items that would make their temporary stay more comfortable. Warm clothing was high on the list of desirable items. He wondered which of his buddies would get to his tent before the guards came to secure his belongings. One would get some nice things, including his leather jacket. He was tired, sad, hungry, sore, worried and confused as he fell into a restless sleep.

The next afternoon, a German guard took him to an office, where he met his interrogator. The German spoke perfect English with no trace of an accent. Christensen was invited to sit down at a table across from the German. He hadn't really spoken to anyone for a couple of days. The interrogator was smiling and friendly. For a moment, Christensen felt relieved and started to let his guard down.

The German passed him a form with "American Red Cross" written at the top and asked him to complete the form. He thought this was how his family would learn of his whereabouts, so he took a pencil and began examining the form. The first few questions asked for his name, rank and serial number. He filled in the answers. The next questions were about his group, base, bomb load and type of aircraft. He passed the form back to his interrogator, explaining he could only provide the information he'd listed. The interrogator slid the form back, saying this was a form for the Red Cross and all the questions must be answered in order for his family to be notified. Christensen again said he wouldn't complete the rest of the form. The light came on for Christensen and he realized the Germans were trying to get military information from him. It wasn't going to work. His interrogator began yelling, telling Christensen that his pilot, Captain Anderson, had already completed the form and everyone must complete the form. Since Christensen didn't even know a Captain Anderson, he realized the German didn't know as much as he thought and handed the form back. The German called him "a damned fool", and told him he would be turned over to the Gestapo. Christensen still refused to complete the form and was taken back to his cell.

That night Christensen was given a bowl of soup. He was kept in the cell for three days and had plenty of time to think about his decision not to provide additional information. He recalled being told during training that once an interrogator was given any information at all, the door would be opened, and they would continue to work on the POW until they had whatever information they wanted. No, it was better not to cooperate at all. After three days he was finally taken from the cell, apprehensive about what was going to happen. He was relieved to be put on a boxcar with other American POWs.

His next stop was a transit camp. Here he was given decent food and a package from the Red Cross. Along with toiletry items, the package contained a sweater, socks and pajamas. He was also issued some additional, much-needed clothing. He lost his boots in the bail-out and had been walking in his electrically heated "booties". The shoes he received were very welcome. He was also given a shirt, pants and a G.I. wool overcoat, which he later credited with saving his life. The Red Cross supplied a brown plastic suitcase, to help carry the items. After a brief stay at the transit camp, he joined other enlisted POW airmen in a crowded boxcar, enroute to his next temporary home at Stalag Luft IV. The POW camp was in what is now Poland, near Gross Tyschow, close to the Baltic Sea. On arrival, Christensen was strip-searched by guards, a demeaning process, and he settled into his new home.

Back at home, families of the airmen were being informed that their sons or husbands were missing; however, the news came slowly, with most of the families receiving telegrams on September 25th. Christensen's mother collapsed when she got the telegram from the Western Union depot agent, who delivered it from the nearby town of Reserve, Montana. The families would later receive a list with the names of all the Boys on the crew, as well as the names and addresses of their next of kin. This allowed them to contact the families of the other Boys if they chose to do so. On October 27th, the families of Canin, Christensen, and

Blodgett received telegrams advising them their sons were POWs, confirmed by the Red Cross.

It was a particularly stressful time for the families of the Boys who were killed. Several wrote to the families of the survivors, hoping to get some word, some spark of hope. On November 28th, Imelda MacDonald, Everett's wife, wrote to Christensen's father.

Dear Mr. Christensen,[25]

I've been wanting to write, but it was only this week that I got your address from Lt. Pat Campolita (bombardier on Christensen's original crew) *who is now home having finished his fifty missions. My husband-Chris probably mentioned him to you as Mac-was on the same crew with your Chris and is missing now on the same flight.*

I have received a lot of encouraging news from several of the fellows that have come home on leave and I know it will relieve your anxiety as it did mine. Lt. Campolita wrote that one of the other pilots of another plane followed our plane for a few minutes after it was hit and saw six or seven chutes open in that time. He also feels sure that all the rest of the chutes followed because the plane still had plenty of altitude.

Lt. Wickman who was the navigator of our crew wasn't flying on the day of the accident and he has been very encouraging. From him we've heard that one of the crew, a Lt. Blodgett, has been reported officially to be a prisoner of war in Germany.

I keep waiting daily to hear that my Mac is safe somewhere in Germany, but the waiting for news has been very hard. You have probably been even more at a loss for news than I, because I have been in touch with Bill's (Bill Lawrence-pilot) *mother and Nitsche's sister since I first received the telegram from the War Department. None of us knew Chris' home address or we*

124

would have written much sooner. If you have had any further news of your son's safety, or news about any members of the crew I would appreciate if you would let me know.

I am expecting a baby any day now and I am hoping to have some news of Mac before I go to the hospital and I pray every day that soon all the boys will be reported safe.

I hope my news helps some, Mrs. Christensen, to give you the encouragement that I feel now. At first I thought the world had come to an end, but with every bit of news I've received, I've had new hope that it will be soon that our boys are home safe and sound.

Please let me hear from you. If I receive any further news, I will let you know right away.

Imelda MacDonald

As their families wondered, or received news, the five survivors settled into POW life. Both camps contained thousands of POWs. The four surviving officers would remain together in the same camp at Barth and Christensen would remain for a while at Stalag Luft IV. In December, Canin was separated from the other POWs in his compound and was housed separately with other Jewish flyers. This was a very stressful change for the Jewish airmen. It was no secret the Nazis hated Jews and now they were being isolated from the other Americans. Fortunately, nothing became of the separation aside from them being housed together, away from the others.

Meanwhile, back at home, the families of the missing Boys searched for answers and were hopeful.

December 5, 1944

Dear Mr. Christensen,[26]

My son, Staff Sgt. Lewis L. Kaplan, was serving with your son T/Sgt. Vernon O. Christensen, on September 13th, the day of the misfortune. My family and I are constantly praying for their safety. Through the suggestion of the Red Cross in Plainfield I wrote to the War Dept requesting the addresses of the next of kin of the boys missing with my son since Sept. 13th.

This letter is written in the hopes that you may have received some word from any other boys in another plane on the same mission who may have seen our boys parachute out of their plane or any other information that might be encouraging.

I would be ever so grateful if you would forward to me any small detail or news you may have received regarding your son and the crew.

May God help us.

Sincerely,
Mrs. Fanny Kaplan

All the families wanted answers. As letters were sent and answered, the families of those missing hoped the families of known survivors would have additional information and words of hope.

December 12, 1944

Dear Mr. Christensen,[27]

I notice that your son was a member of the crew that failed to return Sept. 13-my son also was a crew member. We have been anxious to get some word of them.

My son's wife writes me she had word from several of the crew members of the "Flak Shak" (Matt Hall's original plane and crew) *with which my son went overseas and on combat missions all summer. Lt. Ken Leisure, navigator, wrote he and Sgt. Britton of Atlanta, Ga., one of the gunners, talked to her. Both of them assured her that the plane went down under its own power, they said "under control" I believe. They reported the rumor on the airfield in Italy that two or three of the missing crew are prisoners. If so it will soon be time for the prisoners to be officially reported to the Red Cross in Geneva, who in turn report to the U.S. Army.*

There was a very informative article in the November issue of "Flying" magazine on "Our Captured Airmen" in German prison camps. There was a map showing the location of five of the seven prison camps in Germany and pictures of some of our U. S. pilots in German camp. The article explained regulations as to letters and parcels for prisoners.

If you have any news of any of the crew as to their fate I would appreciate your writing to me and I shall be glad to share any news I happen to have. I hope my next information will be more definite and not just hearsay.

Sincerely,

Mrs. Agnes K. Hall
Mother of Lt. M.W. Hall, copilot

The cold, harsh winter settled in. It was the coldest, most severe European winter in recent history. The boys in Stalag Lufts I and IV received regular updates on the status of the war from crystal radio sets hidden within the camps. Their thoughts were of food. Additional thoughts were not of escape, but the progress of the war. They were hopeful that with the advances of the Americans and Brits in the West, and the Russian advance from the East, the war would soon be over. Escape was virtually impossible. If escape was possible, in their weakened condition their chance for survival was slim.

As the new year began, the Russians continued their march through Poland. Skirmishes and battles were fought as they approached and overran the death camp at Auschwitz. In a wooded area near where Lawrence's plane had crashed, a battle took place. Sgt. Sikora, who mercilessly beat one of the dying airmen from Lawrence's crew, was killed by Russian soldiers. He was buried near the Boys from Lawrence's crew.

In January, large numbers of British POWs arrived at Stalag Luft IV, having been evacuated from other camps to the east. As the Russian armies approached, the Germans evacuated Stalag Luft IV. Their booty, the Allied airmen, would not be liberated by the Russians. Those who were severely ill or seriously injured were evacuated to Stalag Luft I by train. Those able to walk were told, on short notice, to prepare themselves for departure.[28]

On February 6th, those POWs able to walk left Stalag Luft IV on what later became known as The Black March. Christensen donned his entire wardrobe, consisting of socks, underwear, pajamas, shirt, pants, G.I. boots and what he later called his life-saver, the heavy wool G.I. overcoat supplied by the Red Cross. They started out, marching through the snow, each with a Red Cross food parcel. At first they were in three large groups, but the big groups quickly separated into smaller groups. The Red Cross parcels would soon be gone and it was easier to find food for a smaller group. Many thought it would be a short march to a nearby camp, a few days at most. Little did they know.

These POWs would sleep in open fields, bombed out factories, barns, or wherever they were at the end of the day. The time would come when Christensen would have given just about anything to be back at Stalag Luft IV.

There circumstances were different at Stalag Luft I. Since Barth was west of Stalag Luft IV, the Russians were still some distance away and the Germans saw no need to move the POWs. The officers from Lawrence's crew adapted to their routine. They tried to keep themselves busy by reading, playing cards or chess, or taking informal classes taught by their peers. It was a way to pass time and relieve the boredom.

At one point Pratt began having extreme abdominal pain. He feared he was experiencing appendicitis and contacted the British doctor in the camp. The doctor eliminated that possibility, but couldn't determine the cause of the pain. Pratt was sent to a hospital in New Brandenburg by train. The conditions were deplorable at the hospital. Patients were placed on mattresses of straw on wooden benches. Other patients were in much worse shape than Pratt. He heard the gurgling noises, the final death rattles, as patients died in the night. He traded cigarettes for food. Without these, he wouldn't have been fed and would have starved. After testing and a brief stay, he was sent back to Barth. During the return trip several SS troops boarded the train. They made the POWs stand for the remainder of the trip, berating them, threatening them and calling them names. Pratt was glad when he arrived back at camp. His health eventually returned to normal.

Food rations decreased substantially. The Boys stayed in their bunks more, to save energy and to try to stay warm. Conditions became more crowded, with the influx of several thousand POWs from Stalag Luft IV and other camps. To help pass the time, Canin made pencil sketches of his 17 bunkmates in his diary. Others heard of his talent and he was able to trade Red Cross parcels in exchange for making sketches in their diaries. He also made watercolor illustrations of camp life. He quickly earned the nickname "Remmie", short for Rembrandt.

Christensen and his fellow POWs continued walking. All were near starvation. At the beginning of the march, the guards were regular German army, Wehrmacht. Later in the march, these guards were replaced by the Volksturm. These guards were older men or young boys, not considered qualified for combat duty, but still overly matched for the sick, emaciated POWs.

Places and memories mixed as the Boys put one foot in front of the other, one step and one day at a time. Their biggest fear was of not being able to continue. Many came down with dysentery or some other illness. For those with dysentery, word spread through the ranks that charcoal might help them. The believers ate pieces of charcoal, left over from the previous night's fires. They were easily identifiable by the black smudges of charcoal on their mouths and faces.

Keeping their feet in good shape was another major concern. Christensen teamed up with an 8th Air Force buddy from camp, Norman Bunney. They walked every step of the way together, sharing everything, encouraging each other, prodding each other to keep going. They passed through towns and villages, putting one foot in front of the other, hoping to make it through just one more day. They went through Griefeldin, Wollin, Anklem, Swinemunde, Medow, Gultz, Karow, Parchim, Velzen, and Magdeburg. The names and places were endless.

There were other Boys from the 485th on the march, but Christensen didn't know them. Conditions necessitated that he and Norman only concern themselves with each other. They foraged for dandelions and weeds and grass. When walking through farm country, they dug through the dirt, occasionally finding a raw potato to eat, a real bounty. On one occasion they were in a farmyard when a farmer came in with a wagon full of kohlrabi to feed the cattle. The kohlrabi looked awfully good to Christensen. He observed the nearest guard was on the other side of the wagon, so he climbed on the wagon and grabbed a couple of kohlrabi. When he climbed down he was met by the guard, who had seen him. The guard beat Christensen with his rifle butt, knocking him to the ground. As Christensen was being beaten, his only thought was he hoped he wouldn't be beaten so badly that he couldn't continue the march. He was to the point where he would gladly trade a beating for a kohlrabi.

At home, the families of the missing Boys were still waiting for answers. They tried to keep their hopes up, knowing deep down the odds were against the safe return of the other Boys. It wasn't easy.

April 10, 1945

Dear Mrs. Christensen,[29]

It has been quite a while now that I've been wanting to write, but so much has happened I just haven't been able. My baby died when he was just six weeks old and I just went to pieces entirely. There is still no news of my husband's whereabouts. I thought that you must have had a few lines at least from Vernon and I am very interested in any word or hint he might have given of the other boys. I hope that he is in a camp that will be freed by our troops or the Russians very soon.

I am very hopeful that it won't be long now before I hear from my Mac, but I would appreciate any news of Vernon and his whereabouts also.

Sincerely,
Imelda MacDonald

The Russians were approaching Stalag Luft I in April. Many smaller groups of POWs from Stalag Luft IV were being liberated as the Russian troops caught up with them. The German guards kept Christensen's group ahead of the Russian advance.

It was spring now and the weather was considerably warmer. Allied planes ruled the skies. There were occasional strafings and bombings of the airmen from Stalag Luft IV, cases of mistaken identity by the Allies. They were still walking, barely. The food situation was getting worse, not better. They were worn out and most were sick.

On April 13th, the POWs and their guards stopped to take a short break along a dirt road near Belzig. They sat or lay down along the side of the road, exhausted. From the distance a screeching, wailing noise was heard. All eyes were focused on a rise in the road a short distance away. They were trying to determine the source of the noise. As they watched, a ragtag group of British POWs appeared over the rise, led by a bagpiper. It was almost surreal as the group approached.

As they passed, the Brits snapped to attention, marching with the piper. Feelings were mixed amongst the Boys. Some were angry. Here was this group of "limeys" trying to impress a bunch of starving, fellow POWs. Some were just confused, trying to understand what was happening. The anger quickly dissipated as word passed down the line to some of the prisoners. President Roosevelt had died the previous day and the Brits were paying tribute to the fallen leader.

The end had to be near. Sounds of heavy artillery were heard both east and west of the POWs, but the starving airmen wondered how much longer they could continue. There were signs of hope around them, if they could just keep going. One day, as Christensen sat in a ditch alongside the road resting, he heard a plane approaching. He looked up in time to see a P-51 Mustang, down low, possibly on a strafing run, winging its way toward the group. The pilot saw the POWs, rolled the plane on its side and waggled his wings in recognition. What a beautiful sight! The entire group of POWs burst into tears. The pilot had seen them and word would get back. A guard was sitting near Christensen. He turned to Christensen, pulled back the bolt on his rifle, removed the clip of ammunition and handed the clip to Christensen, saying, "Here, you have this for souvenir. Deutschland kaput." (Author's note: Christensen kept the clip for many years, a reminder of that day.)

The end came quietly on the 26th of April. Christensen was sitting in a farm yard with a small group, popping lice that had accumulated in the seams of his clothing. An American jeep drove into the yard, with a major and a sergeant as passengers, driven by another G.I. He'd be forever grateful to his liberators, boys from the 104th Division, the Timberwolves. He turned to his buddy and said, "By God, we made it." And they had. One of the boys in Christensen's group, Bob Tharratt, kept a log of the march, listing the mileage in kilometers. The kilometers totaled 787, nearly 600 miles. They had walked for nearly three months through some of the worst weather in modern European history. More importantly, they had survived.

At Stalag Luft I Blodgett, Pratt, Winter and Canin could hear the sounds of heavy artillery getting closer to Barth at the end of April. On the morning of May 1st, the guards disappeared and left the guard towers empty. The guards had fled, most likely in hopes they could evade capture by the Russians. Senior officers in camp ordered the boys to stay inside the camp. It was just too dangerous outside. They could be mistaken for German soldiers by the approaching Russians.

Liberation came quickly in the form of Russian soldiers on horses and horse-drawn wagons, right out of the 19th Century. Many of them had Mongol features, a surprise to the Americans. The Russians brought in an entertainment group and rounded up cattle from the countryside, for a feast. Arrangements were made for their return to the west.

In the middle of May, the POWs at Barth were marched to the airport, where they were loaded into B-17 Flying Fortresses, 30 men per plane. They were flown to France, where they were taken to Camp Lucky Strike, at Le Havre. Here they were given decent food, checked out by doctors and nursed back to health.

Christensen and his buddies from the march were also flown to France for processing. From there he went to Camp Lucky Strike, where he ate, rested and waited for a ship to take him home. He didn't know the rest of the survivors from his crew were there. In mid-June he boarded the *General Butler*, a troop ship, for the trip across the Atlantic, destination Hampton Roads, Virginia. He became ill while at Camp Lucky Strike. Not wanting to be left behind, he concealed his illness until he was aboard ship, where he was promptly put into the sickbay.

Blodgett, Canin, Winter and Pratt were also enroute home in June. Canin was sick and, like Christensen, was in his ship's sickbay, but recovered by the time he landed in the U.S. He went to Atlantic City on his return home for Rest and Recuperation. Blodgett learned that the pilot from his own crew, Eddie Neitzel, had been killed in Italy. He made a special trip to Milwaukee to visit Neitzel's wife.

When the Boys returned, their families told them that families of the other Boys on the crew were still waiting for answers. They were still listed as MIA, Missing in Action. In some cases, it was left to the survivors to provide answers to the other families. Christensen was extremely ill when his ship docked in Virginia and he would spend a month in the hospital at Camp Patrick Henry.

July 6, 1945

Dear Mr. Christensen,[30]
I know you and Mrs. Christensen are happy that Vernon is back in the States again and will be getting good care from now on. You are probably greatly concerned about both your wife and Vernon, but I'm sure that Vernon will be well again soon and his arrival home will speed your wife's recovery.

I would like very much to go down to Virginia and see Vernon if he is to be in the hospital for quite a while longer. Do you think it would be all right? If talking about what happened to the plane will hurt Vernon and retard his recovery, of course I would give up the idea. From what I have heard the other boys were all strangers and Vernon is the only one who knew Mac.

If you think it will be all right for me to go, please let me know where in Virginia Vernon is, but if you have any doubts I wouldn't want to upset his recovery in any way. In a way, I hope he is home with you already. Being home again will probably do more to make him well and forget what he has been through. Thank you, Mr. Christensen, you have been wonderful.

Sincerely,
Imelda MacDonald

The families of some of the Boys had been corresponding for several months. They shared whatever information was available to them.

July 14, 1945

Dear Mr. Christensen,[31]
Thank you very much for your kindness in writing me about your son's letter as to his own experience in getting off the plane that 13 of Sept, '44. Before your letter came I had received one from your son mailed from the hospital-which I really appreciated! Lt. Blodgett wrote me practically the same story your son tells.

Lt. Canin wrote me that he and your son and Lt. Blodgett stood together at the bomb bay to jump, that he waited till he saw Hall and Lawrence rise to leave their seats to know to abandon ship, for their intercommunication system was out. Canin was the last man to leave the plane as it was going into a spin then and it was with difficulty he jumped clear and made it, only because he was already in position, braced, ready to jump. It was marvelous that he escaped.

We are grateful and thankful to God that five of the crew were spared to return and bring us word of how it happened. It is a comfort to read the boys' letters-their faith in God and His providence and the knowledge that our sons are in His keeping is our consolation. Indeed, I know the poem "High Flight". My son sent the words from his first cadet training school in Montgomery, Alabama. I heard Nelson Eddy sing it over the radio recently. It has been set to music. The thought is beautiful. With best wishes for your son's speedy recovery.

Sincerely,
Agnes Hall
(Matt Hall's mother)

The Boys hadn't forgotten those who were left behind or their families. Imelda MacDonald visited Vernon Christensen in the hospital, where he remained for a month, recovering from a severe case of what was probably hepatitis. Painful as it was, he shared the details of those final moments over Auschwitz. It was wrenching for both of them. For Christensen, it was reliving the terror and grieving the loss of Mac and his other buddies. For Imelda, it was hearing the details of her husband's death and being forced to confront the fact that her Mac would not be coming home. This, coupled with the recent death of her baby boy, was nearly too much to bear. Painful as it was, she was grateful to Christensen for sharing. A couple of days later, Christensen got a get well card from Marcella Eggers, William's mother.

July 17, 1945

Dear Friend,[32]

There is little we can say, only we are glad to know you are back and hope you will be yourself before long and restored to your family's bosom. Mrs. Hall sent me a copy of your letter. I also received letters from Winter, Canin, and Blodgett. Right now, we know they want to enjoy their return home and relax.

Some day when you boys feel up to it, I would like to know the positions of crew and where flak hit. Best wishes for health and happiness.

Mrs. M. Eggers

Blodgett visited Eggers' sister. The Boys who returned were able to provide some comfort to the families of their buddies who would not return. Nitsche's parents visited Christensen at the hospital. Once again, he painfully recounted the details of the mission, so they would know what happened. He, MacDonald, Nitsche and Lawrence had been together since their original crew was formed. Now, except for him, they were all gone. Christensen was well enough to return home to Montana in August.

This would normally be the end of the story; however, a series of events transpired to continue the story and honor the Boys from this crew and from the 485th Bomb Group, for they were not forgotten.

In 1992, Donald Rice, then Secretary of the Air Force, made an official visit to Poland. He was told of a monument erected by some townspeople between Zygodowice and Wadowice, just a few miles from Auschwitz. The monument honored an American bomber crew that was shot down there in September, 1944. From here the story unfolds, tying it to those events in 1944. Rice took an interest and requested follow-up information to learn more about this crew and their mission.

As the search for information began, the Air Force learned these Boys from Venosa had not been forgotten by the Polish people. After the six Boys were buried, the Poles continued to place flowers on the common grave, at personal risk.

In 1947, the U.S. military returned and disinterred the remains of the six Boys. Stefan Wiktor, a local resident, recalls that an American car came to Zygodowice in 1947. The car had a white star on it and American soldiers in it. They asked him where the Americans were buried and he took them to the gravesite.[33]

Because Sgt. Sikora and other German soldiers had taken all identification and personal items, the identity of the remains was unknown. Through careful interviews with people who had witnessed the event, the date of the crash was determined to be September 13, 1944. Military records were searched to determine which B-24s from the 15th Air Force were shot down in the region on that date, and which Americans flyers from these planes hadn't been returned or otherwise identified. Medical files of these airmen were obtained and the painstaking process of forensic identification began. All six were positively identified. Their remains were returned to the U.S. or interred in a U.S. military cemetery in western Europe.

As the years passed the Boys and the crash site were not forgotten. When Russian domination ended, the locals made plans to erect a permanent monument at the site. A local man, Zygmunt Kraus, had taken an interest in the crew of the downed bomber. He collected pieces of the downed aircraft with the intention of having the items on display in a private museum. Kraus petitioned the President of Poland, requesting the Polish Veterans Cross be presented to the survivors of the crew and to the families of the six who died that day.

Back at home, Dan Mortensen, an Air Force Historian, was assigned to research the matter and attempt to locate any of the survivors still living. He located Winter, Pratt, Christensen and Blodgett. All were invited to the Polish Embassy in Washington D.C., where they were presented the Polish Veterans Cross. Two sisters of Matt Hall were also located and they were presented his medal at the ceremony. Paul Canin could not be located and was presumed deceased. Families of the other crewmen that perished could not be found.

In 1994, the survivors were invited to Poland for a ceremony commemorating the 50th anniversary of the event. Christensen attended, representing the crew and the other Boys from Venosa. It was an emotional event and a clear indication they have not been forgotten. The inscription on the monument reads, "On this spot on 13 September, 1944, six American airmen died in a battle for Polish freedom". Once the names of the crew were given to the Poles, the names of those who died were added to the inscription on the monument.

42. The memorial site at Zygodowice

Paul Canin was located in 2003, alive and well.[34] He has now received his medal. Zygmunt Kraus maintains his small museum in Wadowice, dedicated to the Boys from Venosa who went down that day. The U.S. Air Force provided him with additional information, photos and items for his exhibit. It is now a local tourist attraction, just across the alley from another local point of interest, Pope John Paul II's birthplace.

✪ The Story ✪

This story gripped me. There is no other way to describe it. It took hold of me and took me with it. The journey took me to Poland to a memorial ceremony for the crew. It gripped me harder when we located witnesses who saw the plane fall near them, witnesses who saw the dead airmen on the ground, a witness who carefully buried them and watched his friends plead with the Germans for a decent burial, and another witness who was caught by the Germans placing flowers on the gravesite and threatened with imprisonment at Auschwitz if she did this again.

The grip tightened when I visited the field where the plane crashed and pictured the big bomber falling from the sky. When I saw the fresh flowers and burning candles at the memorial site, I asked if they were for the memorial ceremony being held the next day. The answer, almost indignant, was that fresh flowers and burning candles are a permanent part of the memorial, maintained by locals and schoolchildren in this poor farming community, in honor of this crew and other Americans who flew over Poland in WWII.

It started out as just a story. I thought it would be of interest to include a story about a little known mission to the oil refinery outside the notorious concentration camp and of the crew lost near the target. I phoned Chris Christensen, one of the gunners, in Montana. We talked for a while and he sent his memoirs. As I read them and learned more about the mission I became convinced the story of this crew must be included, but I had many unanswered questions.

I wondered what happened to the radar navigator, Irving P. Canin. Chris knew Canin made it to the ground safely. He met Canin for the first time the morning of the mission, but had a vague recollection of seeing Canin on the ground after they were captured, and of knowing Canin was the last one to safely leave the plane. Assumptions were made that Canin was dead and that he may have been killed by the S.S., due to his Jewish heritage.

I began my search for more information. I wasn't as convinced as others were of Canin's death because I could find no death records. Ultimately I found him, living less than 20 miles from me. He uses his middle name now, Paul, which contributed to the difficulty in finding him and is likely the reason the Air Force couldn't locate him in their search in the early 90's. Paul now has his medal from the Polish government and knows the rest of the story.

In 2004, I invited Chris Christensen to visit my wife and me in California. We arranged for Paul and Chris to meet again. It was a wonderful reunion. Although they had only been together for one brief day in their lives, they shared a commonality of experience that few of us can understand.

While making preparations for Chris's visit, I spoke with a friend, Bob Tharratt, who was in Stalag Luft IV when Chris was there. Bob and I have become friends during the past two years and I used Bob's recollections for some of the background information in this story. I asked Bob if he knew Chris and he said he didn't. Chris said the same thing about Bob. They were in different compounds and it would seem they would have had little chance of crossing paths among the thousands of POWs. Still, I thought there was a small chance they had been together.

I continued looking for a link that may have joined them, questioning both of them further. Both assured me they hadn't met. As I reflect back on it, Chris and Bob were both probably just a little annoyed that I wouldn't drop my search for a connection between them. Both were anxious to get together during Chris's visit, because they still shared the experience of Stalag Luft IV and the horrible march.

In my search for a connection I recalled one unusual happening that Chris described to me, the almost surreal sighting of the bagpiper on the march. Chris had no memory of where or when this occurred on the march. In my next meeting with Bob, in a last ditch effort to find a connection, I asked Bob if he remembered a bagpiper on the march. He just stared at me. It was almost as if he had seen a ghost. Then Bob told me what he saw that day in April. His observations were identical to what Chris had seen, but Bob had more specific information to include in the story. Both agreed that I finally found the link. Once again the story gods were in my corner.

When Chris and Bob met during Chris's visit to California, it became increasingly obvious they had walked every step of the march together in the same small group. One would start a story and the other would finish it. They didn't know each other on the march but they know each other now. Each has a new friend.

Burl Jackson, a man who was on Lewis Kaplan's original crew, recently sent me a couple of letters from 1944. One was a letter from Kaplan's sister, Rebecca Uslan, written to Jackson after Kaplan was shot down. For some reason Burl thought I should have the letter. Armed with this information I began my search and located Rebecca in New Jersey. She finally knows what happened to her brother over Poland that day. More importantly, she and her family know he is not forgotten. In the near future the family will receive the medal issued by the Polish government in recognition of his service and sacrifice.

The information in this story is as complete as I could make it, but it's still not finished for me. I made a promise to Chris Christensen to locate the families of the other three men on the crew that day, so they can have the comfort of knowing that the Polish people have not forgotten. Those still to be located are the families of William Lawrence (Little Rock, Arkansas), Everett MacDonald (Everett, Massachusetts) and Art Nitsche (Southington, Connecticut). I could use some help from the story gods in completing this part of the story.

JW

142

NOTES & REFERENCES

[1] Bill Herblin specifically recalled this briefing when interviewed by the author on 10/08/04. He described the camp (actually two camps-Auschwitz and Birkenau) as being common around oil refineries and other industrial targets where the Germans used forced labor to build and maintain the sites. He described his horror when he learned after the war, with the general public, of what had occurred at some of these "labor camps".

[2] The perceptions of Lawrence as a pilot were obtained from Colonel Dan Sjodin, 831st Sqdn C.O. during an interview at Little Rock, Arkansas on 9/17/03.

[3] This "officer buddy" is Jack Breen, 831st Sqdn navigator from Jess Ledbetter's crew. The comment was made during a conversation with the author at Little Rock, Arkansas on 9/20/03.

[4] The crew background information on Hall is from various newspaper articles supplied by the Robert Hickman family and from personal conversations with Hickman on 9/18/03 and 9/19/03 at Little Rock, Arkansas. Hickman was the tail gunner on Hall's original crew and was also injured in the referenced mission.

[5] Frank Pratt provided this information during a phone interview on 7/11/04.

[6] Dan Blodgett provided this personal information, along with details about navigation, during a phone interview on 1/25/04.

[7] Paul Canin provided this information during an interview on 1/20/04 in Berkeley, California.

[8] John Jones, 831st Sqdn pilot, provided this information about Eggers in a 2/24/04 email.

[9] Burl Jackson provided the background information on Kaplan in a letter dated 3/23/04. Jackson and Kaplan were both gunners on William Montoux's crew. Montoux was taken off flying status after a particularly rough mission to Vienna in June of 1944 and the crew was broken up. Supplemental info on Kaplan is from phone interviews with Rebecca Uslan, Kaplan's sister and Leslie Uslan, Kaplan's niece in April, 2005.

[10] Christensen knew Nitsche and MacDonald very well, having trained with them, and having flown his missions with them. He gave this background information during an interview on 1/19/04.

[11] Paul Canin related this in a 1/20/04 interview in Berkeley, California.

[12] Mission summary from 485th Bomb Group Narrative Mission Report, dated 9/13/44.

[13] Christensen's observations are from interviews on 9/17/03 and 1/19/04 and from his privately published memoirs *By God, We Made It!*

[14] The remainder of the story concerning Pratt and Winter is summarized from a phone interview with Frank Pratt on 7/11/04.

[15] The details of the remainder of Canin's story are from *Some World War II Memoirs* by Paul Canin and from interviews with him on 1/15/04 in Walnut Creek, California and 1/19/04 in Berkeley, California.

[16] Blodgett and Canin specifically recalled this sequence of events when both were interviewed. Christensen could only recall part of it, most likely due to the lack of oxygen at high altitude.

[17] What occurred on the ground with the dead airmen, and the events concerning the crash and crash site were obtained from copies of 10/20/47 interviews of Polish witnesses by the U.S. Army Graves Registration Unit, contained in the Individual Deceased Personnel File of Captain William C. Lawrence.

[18] From 9/14/04 interview.

[19] From *Wspomnienia wojenne z Zygodowic i okolicy z lat 1939-1945.*

[20] From author's interview with Stefan Wiktor on 9/14/04

[21] From author's interview with Maria Skrzynska on 9/14/04 and from 10/2/47 interview summaries by Graves Registration Unit.

[22] Ibid

[23] Some of the survivors' stories about what occurred immediately after their capture differ, but on most points are very similar.

[24] The remainder of Christensen's story was related in a series of interviews in Walnut Creek, California, between 1/14/04 and 1/20/04.

[25] From Christensen family collection

[26] Ibid

[27] Ibid

[28] The events which are related in this story about "The Black March" were obtained from an interview with Chris Christensen and Bob Tharratt, in Walnut Creek, California on 1/17/04. Bob Tharratt was a ball gunner on a B-17, 338 BS, 96BG, 8th Air Force, shot down over Nurnberg on 9/10/44. Tharratt and Christensen met for the first time on 1/15/04. Both were at Stalag Luft IV and were on the march together, in the same group. Their collective memories provided the details of the experience on the march. Also referenced were Bob Tharratt's self-published memoirs, particularly his daily log of the march.

[29] from Christensen family collection

[30] Ibid

[31] Ibid

[32] Ibid

[33] From author's 9/14/04 interview with Wiktor.

[34] The author located Canin, living in Berkeley, California. Christensen and Canin established phone contact and the two finally met in person in January, 2004.

Some Would Be Home for Christmas

On September 24, 1944, the British began their invasion of Greece by plane, glider and ship. The 15th Air Force was called in to assist and the 485th and 460th Bomb Groups were assigned to bomb the west marshaling yard at Salonika, on the northeast coast of Greece. The 485th would lead the mission with the 460th trailing behind. The thirty-two planes of the 485th rendezvoused with a similar number of aircraft from the 460th over Spinazzola, Italy around 9:20 a.m. and began their flight to Greece. This was the only time during the war the 485th would bomb a Greek target.

Flak on the bomb run was intense and accurate. 1st Lt. Robert Hegmann's plane, in the #2 position on the right wing of the group leader, was hit with the first burst. The #3 engine burst into flames. The plane maintained level flight for a few seconds, with flames burning along the left wing and fuselage. Slowly it fell out of the formation, losing altitude and suddenly exploded, separating into three flaming pieces. Witnesses in other planes saw no parachutes.

2nd Lt. James Cameron's 829th Squadron crew, flying in the #5 position directly behind Hegmann, was in trouble. Their bomber was hit by pieces of Hegmann's exploding plane before Cameron and copilot Flight Officer Alex Vroblesky could take evasive action. They dove the plane to get away from other burning debris. When Cameron pulled back on the controls, the plane didn't respond.[1] One of the wing tips was on fire. Cameron engaged the auto pilot, hoping the controls would respond, but the plane still didn't react. Still in a dive, Cameron again pulled back on the controls; again there was no response. He ordered the crew to bail out, and then jumped himself.

Several other planes were hit by the intense flak. Men in at least three other planes were wounded by flak. Twelve other planes were damaged before they were out of range of the big German guns, three with major damage.

The Boys in Hegmann's plane didn't have a chance. Those inside felt the plane buck, then break apart. In the rear of the plane the tail gunner, Tech. Sgt. Dale Morrison, felt the plane falling. The back of the plane, now separated from the front, was on fire from an earlier hit in the bomb bay. He struggled to get out of his turret and saw Tech. Sgt. Tom White and Tech. Sgt. Walter Stone on the floor. Both men were waist gunners and lay on the floor unconscious. Morrison quickly located their parachutes, hooked the chutes to their harnesses and pushed them out of the burning plane, pulling their ripcords as he pushed them out. Both parachutes opened, but caught fire and burned and the gunners fell to earth. Morrison jumped behind them and his parachute barely had time to open before he hit the ground.

Somehow 1st Lt. Joe Hackler, the bombardier, also managed to escape from the burning bomber after it broke apart. Both Hackler and Morrison landed in an open field northwest of Salonika. They were captured immediately by German troops in the area as they removed their parachute harnesses. Both were taken to a hospital and treated for burns and other injuries and then were taken to the political prison in Salonika. The other eight members of their crew were killed.[2]

Cameron's crew fared better. As the plane spiraled downward, the Boys began leaving the plane.[3] The navigator, 2nd Lt. William Meeks, bailed out through the bomb bay, followed by Vroblesky, the copilot, and the top turret gunner, Staff Sgt. Wilson Leon. Cameron also left through the bomb bay.

2nd Lt. William McLean, the bombardier, went to the aid of the nose gunner, Cpl. Orville Kingsberg, still in his turret. McLean pulled Kingsberg from the turret, snapped on his parachute and looked toward the cockpit. Seeing no legs or feet where the pilots normally sat, McLean realized the pilots had left their positions to bail out. The plane was still in a dive as McLean pulled Kingsberg from his turret and pulled the emergency release lever for the nose wheel doors. He wrapped Kingsberg's fingers around the ripcord and pushed him out the nose wheel opening and then jumped himself.[4]

Staff Sgt. Robert Burling, the engineer/waist gunner and Cpl. Homer Jones, the radio operator/waist gunner bailed out the rear of the plane, along with Cpl. Ed Czakoczi, the ball gunner and Cpl. Reginald Lyons, the tail gunner. All made it safely out of the aircraft.

Meeks landed in the hills north of Salonika. German soldiers who manned a nearby flak gun battery captured him immediately. After a brief stop at the German headquarters in Salonika, he was taken to the political prison in Salonika and placed in solitary confinement. Hackler and Morrison joined him at the prison.

Cameron was hanging in his parachute, watching the ground approach, near the town of Lankadas. As he neared the ground, he saw two farmers running in his direction. He landed hard, spraining his ankle, but quickly got up, took off his parachute and hid in a nearby ditch. The two farmers found him and he tried to explain that he was an American airman. They motioned for him to follow and all three started walking. About five minutes later they motioned for him to hide in a vineyard. He found a hiding place and the farmers left. Cameron injured an ankle in the bail out and the ankle was hurting.

Fifteen minutes later two boys approached Cameron and motioned for him to follow them. He followed them for about thirty minutes and then stopped, due to severe pain in his ankle. The boys left and he hid alongside a creek. About two hours later the boys returned with a mule. Cameron got on the mule and rode until dark, going into the hills, where he hid for the night.

The other Boys who bailed out landed near the town of Lankadas. Except for Vroblesky, all were immediately captured. Vroblesky ran into a ravine, but the place was swarming with German soldiers and he was captured twenty minutes after landing. All eight were searched for weapons and taken to military police headquarters at Lankadas. Here they were strip-searched. After the search their personal items were returned to them. Individual interrogations followed. Most of the questions were about personal family matters. After the prisoners refused to answer the questions or give up information, they were not questioned further.

All were taken to the outskirts of Salonika by car. Under guard, the enlisted men were marched through town. German soldiers and Greek civilians lined the streets. The Greeks cheered as the POWs walked through the streets. The Americans were then loaded into trucks and taken to a German officers' quarters just outside of Salonika. The eight airmen were fed at the officers' mess and put in a room with double bunks, straw mattresses and blankets. The room was guarded throughout the night by a solitary soldier.

The next morning they were taken to a Luftwaffe barracks near the airfield. Here they were treated very well, given good food and allowed to shower. They stayed at the airfield until September 28th and were then taken by truck to the political prison where they joined their navigator, Meeks and the two Boys from the other crew, Hackler and Morrison.

On the evening of the September 28th, all eleven Boys were taken by truck to a freight yard several miles outside of Salonika. They were put in a freight car, along with two Russian airmen, fourteen German soldiers who were evacuees from Crete and several German guards. The Russians were taken off the train a couple of days later. The POWs were told they were going north, to Budapest. This was the beginning of a long trek. They were given canned rations to eat along the way.

While the other Boys were adjusting to captivity, Cameron made his way further into the hills, away from Salonika and the populated areas, aided by Greek civilians and Partisans. He finally reached a village where he would spend the next four weeks. By this time the British were advancing in Greece. Partisans sent a car to pick him up and he rode back to Salonika, now free of German control. While at Salonika, the Red Cross informed Cameron that the others from his crew were POWs. A British Wellington bomber picked him up at Salonika and flew him to Athens Greece, where a British C-47 took him back to Bari. Cameron arrived back in Italy on November 8th.

As Cameron was escaping into the hills of Greece, the train carrying the other Boys journeyed north. It stopped often on sidings, allowing troop trains and those containing important supplies for the German war effort to pass. They spent more time on the sidings than traveling and even reversed course a couple of times. Their train appeared to be some sort of a refugee train, taking German troops and pro-Axis civilians in the opposite direction of the British advance. While stopped along the way, they ate their canned rations, soup, and other food provided by the Germans.

On the 4th of October, the train pulled into the station at Skopje. The POWs were taken off the train and marched to the Turkish prison where just a few months earlier Major Walter

Smith's crew had been interrogated. They were not subjected to the interrogations suffered by the earlier crew and the next morning they marched back to the train station, where they boarded another northbound train. They continued their slow journey, still spending much of their time on sidings as other trains passed. The days were boring and seemed endless, interrupted a couple of times by strafing attacks from Bulgarian planes that had recently joined the Allied cause.

On the 18th of October the train stopped at Mitrovica. The railway lines had been damaged south of Belgrade and the train could not make it through the area. The Boys were taken to a temporary POW camp. The camp appeared to have once been a school, although there was no doubting its purpose now. Barbed wire surrounded the camp and the perimeter was patrolled by German guards. The camp contained about 1200 Italian POWs, along with Russian and Bulgarian POWs. The Boys set up camp in a vacant house. There were no beds, so they slept on the floor, using straw mattresses.

Their quarters were full of bugs. Food consisted of soup and black bread, both in short supply. All lost weight. Some of the Italian POWs worked at the German dump. They stole food from the dump and shared it with the Americans, which supplemented their meager rations and kept them from starving. They got no exercise and were not allowed out of the compound. While at the camp several British POWs joined them.

On November 5th, the Germans began to evacuate the camp. The new plan was for all the POWs to walk to Germany. The Italian POWs and most of the Russian POWs were first to leave. The Boys, five British POWs, one Bulgarian officer and four Russian airmen left together, accompanied by twelve German and twelve Italian Fascist guards and three police dogs. They were followed by several horse-drawn wagons.

By the second day they had walked about 37 kilometers. They stopped to camp along the road and a small band of Chetniks passed through their camp. The Chetniks stopped to shake hands with the Boys and the other POWs, unchallenged by the German and Italian guards. The next morning at daybreak the Chetniks returned in force. No shots were fired, but they demanded the POWs be turned over to them. The Germans hesitated, and then turned one of the dogs loose on the Chetniks. The POWs took off running, scattering in various directions.

The Chetniks quickly rounded up the POWs and killed the German and Italian guards. The group left for a Chetnik headquarters where they met the Chetnik commander, Major Markovitch. During the next two weeks the Boys would stay in the same general area. As the Germans retreated, Allied planes strafed the roads and railways. The freed British POWs were Special Operations types. They set to work collecting explosives, intending to destroy the retreating German trains and the tracks that carried them. They set booby traps along the rails and blew up train tracks and bridges, trying to slow the German retreat. All the Boys were given Italian carbines and ammunition.

The Boys heard pro-Allied Bulgarian troops had advanced to Mitrovica. On November 23rd, they decided to leave. They were anxious to get back to Italy. While preparing to leave the farmhouse where they were staying, they were warned that the Germans were nearby. They took off, climbing several small mountains in the area. They returned later in the day when it was safe.

On the 24th the Boys left, setting off on foot for a nearby railway station. They found the tracks destroyed by retreating Germans, so they continued walking. Late in the day they met a Bulgarian cavalry patrol. The Bulgarians took them to their headquarters to spend the night. The next day they walked to Mitrovica.

During the next few days the Boys made their way to Sofia, mostly traveling in Bulgarian army trucks. They passed through recent battlefields, where evidence of the fighting was still very visible. By the 29th of November they were within 30 kilometers of Sofia. The Boys stayed at a military complex and were prohibited from entering Sofia, the Bulgarian capitol. The Russians were in charge and they made all the rules. The Boys wanted to get to the American Mission or the British Mission in Sofia. Either would do. They were now literally caught in the midst of some "red tape".

Finally, on December 4th, the Boys received official permission to enter Sofia. Two staff cars arrived to take them to the American college, where they were given rooms. The group relaxed in Sofia, gaining back some of their strength. On December 25th, they were finally given permission by the Russians to return to Italy. A C-47 arrived at the airport and they were flown back to Bari, Italy. Not quite "home" by Christmas, but it was a close second.

Homecoming was bittersweet for the two survivors from Hegmann's crew, Hackler and Morrison. Both felt a duty to provide answers to family members of those who were killed over Salonika. The following is an excerpt from a letter Lt. Joe Hackler sent to the mother of Thomas White, one of the gunners on Hegmann's crew. White was on his 50th mission when he died in the air over Salonika.

February 7, 1945

My dear Mrs. White[5],

Maybe you will recall my name; I am the bombardier who was on Tom's crew that fateful day over Greece. I wanted to write you just what I know about that mission; although I'm afraid what I have to say is not cheerful. Even kind letters are rather cold; I wish I could just sit down and have a long warm, friendly talk with you about Tom.

You see, the plane got a direct hit and blew into many pieces. I am almost positive that it killed the other members of the crew almost instantly. Only two of us were able to get out, and that was due to a great miracle. We had extreme difficulty in getting out for, as I mentioned before, the plane was in many pieces and it just happened that the tail gunner (Sgt. Morrison) and I were lucky enough not to be near the direct hit which was very near the center of the plane. I mention this merely to substantiate my belief that none of the others were able to get out. Tom was in the waist position with Sgt. Stone as we went over the target that day and both of them were doing a good job manning their guns. But I'm afraid they just couldn't find a chance to get out. When Morrison and I floated to the ground we didn't have the chance to inspect the bits of plane which had scattered over the countryside for conclusive evidence that the others were killed (the Germans were right on the spot to pick us up) but it is our truthful opinion, Mrs. White, that Tom could not possibly survive. Maybe the War Department has not written you the final word, but do not blame them too much, for they give only the information they know is correct, and since this is only an opinion, they may wait quite a while before telling you, hoping for another miracle. But I do not expect anything that good. I hope you will excuse me for being so direct but I know your long days have been filled with expectations for word of some kind, and I am doing that which I think is right. I know my wife would want any bit of information she could get.

And I wanted to tell you how much the boys loved Tom. Seems like Tom was the life of our outfit. He always had a kind word; he always had a wisecrack for the others. We officers enjoyed him so much we visited their tent often, and they came over to see us a lot, too. On missions we always chatted and joked over the interphone until just before the target, forgetting what lay ahead. Tom seemed always to be the one to lead the thoughts; he was older than the others as you may already know (I was the next oldest, 27). But I never knew anyone to fit into a group of boys like Tom did-just perfectly. And every time he got a package from home he'd call all the guys together for a celebration. He was just the nicest, kindest person I've known. I've thought of him many times since then, hoping for a miracle that somehow he was safe, but Mrs. White, I just can't twist my hopeful expectations enough to have that consoling thought. Somehow I just can't say the things I feel about Tom. He was as close a friend as I ever had anywhere, and you know what that means. I'm not much good at writing things like this. But I wanted you to know, first, what I knew about the mission, and secondly, just how much all the boys who knew Tom loved him. I'm having a hard time trying to express my belief about the boys and still trying to spare you the pains of grief which I know you feel now. Seems like I can almost feel for you. When I got back to Italy and returned to the base, I just couldn't feel right there without them—there was such an empty feeling that I wanted to get away. I finished my necessary business as quickly as I could and left. I shall never forget those boys.

I know this letter comes as a shock, and I know it won't lessen your grief, but I know you are proud to know that Tom was so well liked. He made our every mission and our every day seem shorter and easier.

And now I'm trying to find a good ending for such a cold message. But Eloise says there isn't any such thing as a good ending for this kind of letter. And I know there isn't. If I can answer any question at all for you, please do write. May God bless you, Mrs. White, and keep you strong through the years.

Your friend,
Joe Hackler

Sgt. Dale Morrison also wrote to Mrs. White, providing her with more specific details of what happened to her son.

April 27, 1945

Dear Mr. And Mrs. White:

I returned home on furlough the day Mother received the letter from you concerning Tom. I can't find words enough to express my sympathy to you at such a critical time as this. Tom was a very close friend of mine and I pray every day that in some way or other he will come back to you. What I am about to tell you I only wish wasn't true but I know you will want to know exactly what happened.

We were the very first plane over the target and one of the first bursts of flak gave us a direct hit in the bomb bay, ripping our ship into 4 parts. We started falling straight down immediately. Our plane was a mass of flames due to the mixing of oxygen and gasoline. I got out of the tail turret after quite a long struggle and managed to get over to Tom and Stone, the engineer. They were both unconscious. I put their parachutes on them and threw them out of the plane, pulling their rip cord as they left the ship. I put Tom out first, but the flames had burned his chute too badly and when it opened, everything seemed all right until suddenly his entire parachute burst into flames. I then threw Stone out in the same manner, but his chute also burned immediately. I too would have went as they did had I not been nearly to the ground when I jumped. My chute had an extremely large hole in it.

Mr. And Mrs. White, I want to express my deepest sympathy and sorrow to you and I want you to know that I too have shared much grief with you that is unknown to anyone. God claims all of us in time, but in time of war it is expected to be quicker to some of us. Your son has gone like a hero and I am sure it is the way Tom would like to go. He finished his job like a real man would. That was our 50th and last mission when fate struck with all its might and brutality. Yes, Tom gave his life so that his loved ones might live on and Tom would have wanted them to.

I am very sorry I am the one to have to send such dreaded news to one's family that meant so much to me solely by raising a son like Tom. Tom meant much more to me than just a friend, but again I say, God must take all of us in time and in war time it is at a much quicker rate.

Goodbye Mr. And Mrs. White, and may God bless you and keep you well through this terrible hated tragedy. If there is anything more I can tell you I would be more than glad to. My deepest sorrow and sympathy to you.

 T/Sgt Dale E. Morrison

For some, there was no happy ending.

42A. Lt. Robert Hegmann crew, 829ᵗʰ B.S. Back row, left to right: Joe Hackler, bombardier; Bryson Watts, copilot; Robert Hegmann, pilot and Edgar Christian, navigator. Front row, far left, Cecil Smith, second from left, Foster Chapman; far right, Dale Morrison. The other men in the photo are unknown

42B. Lt. Jim Cameron crew, 829ᵗʰ B.S. Back row, left to right: Jim Cameron, pilot; Alex Vroblesky, copilot; William McLean, bombardier and William Meeks, navigator. Front row, left to right: Wilson Leon, waist gunner, Homer Jones, radio operator/waist gunner; Orville Kingsberg, nose gunner; Edward Czakoczi, ball gunner; Reginald Lyons, tail gunner and James Dixon, flight engineer. (Christian, Chapman and Dixon were not on this mission.)

42C. Thomas White

The Story

In the fall of 2001, just a few weeks after my first book came out, I met Bill MacLean at a bomb group reunion. We had a private conversation, away from the crowd. He knew of some of my research and said he had been a POW, but had escaped. He was interested in finding any official records of the mission, particularly about his crew. MacLean told me he and his crew escaped several weeks after their capture. He asked if I could obtain additional information for him. I agreed to try to help him.

It seemed incredible to me that a large group of airmen could have escaped, especially after being in captivity for that length of time. The story really caught my interest. I began searching the 485th Bomb Group microfilm records, but couldn't seem to find what I was looking for. Several months after I began my search I stumbled upon the Escape Statements for Bill's crew. I had also requested additional information from the Air Force Historical Research Agency at Maxwell Air Force Base. They sent the Missing Air Crew Report, which provided more specific information.

I sent Bill the records I obtained. I wasn't aware that he was writing his memoirs of his experience. I collected my information, intending to write the story about this group of airmen, focusing on all of the men who went down over Salonika that day in September. I met Bill again in Washington D.C. in the fall of 2004. At that time I learned of his writing, based on a diary he kept during his captivity.

I was contacted in 2004 by a Canadian woman, Mary Gordon. She wanted to learn more about her great uncle, Tom White, who was killed while flying with Lt. Hegmann's crew on the Salonika mission. I provided her with information from my research. She graciously supplied me with the transcripts of two letters from the two survivors of her great uncle's crew. Just reading the contents of the letters was a humbling experience for me and seemed a fitting way to end the story.

JW

NOTES AND REFERENCES

[1] Cameron documented his actions in his Escape Statement, 485th Bomb Group records. The information about his bailout and subsequent evasion came from this source.

[2] The MACR listed ten men on the plane that day, including two navigators. Since no top turret gunner was listed on the roster, one could assume the second navigator also served as a turret gunner. The members of the crew killed that day were 1st Lt. Robert Hegmann (pilot), 1st Lt. Bryson Watts (copilot), 1st Lt. Marvin Weiner (navigator), 2nd Lt. Everett Latham (navigator), Tech Sgt. Walter Stone (flight engineer), Tech Sgt. Thomas White (waist gunner), S/Sgt. Joseph Cullen (nose gunner), and S/Sgt. Cecil Smith (ball gunner).

[3] The information about the exits of Cameron's crew came from Individual Casualty Questionnaires for Cameron's crew contained in Missing Air Crew Report #8951, 15th Air Force records.

[4] The specifics about McLean's bail-out and subsequent capture were obtained from his privately published memoirs *Mission Log from the 'Milk Run' to Freedom*.

[5] Letters courtesy of Mary Gordon.

Rescued by our Friends

I n October of 1944, the Germans were retreating from Greece, through Albania and into Yugoslavia. The Russians occupied Romania and Bulgaria and were pushing into Yugoslavia from the east. The Soviets and Partisans captured Belgrade on the 10th and the Brits and Greeks captured Athens on the 14th. Russian forces quickly occupied Nis, Yugoslavia, after it was vacated by the Germans. In Italy, the Boys were flying regularly. On October 16th, they were scheduled to fly a mission to Austria.

One of the Boys had just recently returned to flying status. Staff Sgt. Billy Culver, a 19 year-old gunner, had already gone down once while returning from Ploesti on August 24, 1944. He was on his seventh mission. They lost three engines and fuel tanks and fuel lines were hit and leaking. After "bombs away", two of the gas tanks were hit, causing more damage. Lt. Francis Lozita, the pilot, headed for Yugoslavia. The crew threw out everything that wasn't bolted down, including guns and ammo and made it into Yugoslavia. The entire crew bailed out safely over the Yugoslavian countryside when it was apparent they couldn't make the coast. They were lucky and all were picked up by Partisans. All except the pilot were evacuated fifteen days later after a lot of walking, hiding and avoiding German patrols. Lozita suffered a broken leg and remained in Yugoslavia a while longer, but was eventually evacuated.[1]

43. Bill Culver

Lozita's crew was split up after their return. They went to rest camp and the crew was broken up on their return. Culver was assigned to fly missions with other crews whenever they needed an extra gunner. October 16th was one of those days and it was his third mission since returning to duty. The day before, he was playing football with some of the Boys when one of the gunners injured his leg. Culver didn't know he was replacing the injured gunner until he was awakened in his tent the next morning.

Culver didn't know any of the Boys on this crew. He hadn't flown with any of them and he never knew all their names. 1st Lieutenant Richard Boehme was the pilot and 2nd Lt. Merwin Jacobson was the copilot. 2nd Lt. Bob Bishop was the navigator and 2nd Lt. Richard Weintritt was the bombardier. The right waist gunner/flight engineer was Cpl. Elvis Waisath. The radio operator and left waist gunner was Cpl. Abe Goldman. The other gunners were Cpl. Kenneth Lohr in the ball turret, Cpl. Harold Oliver in the nose turret and Cpl. Bob Brown in the tail turret. They just needed a gunner to replace the top turret gunner and Culver drew the assignment.

The target was in Austria. Culver learned during briefing they were flying in the "slot" or #4 position, directly behind the formation leader. He had a good view of things ahead of him while

160

44. Lt. Boehme's crew. Lt. Weintritt is kneeling on the left and Lt. Boehme is kneeling, far right. The other members of the crew aren't individually identified.

enroute to the target. Waisath monitored the fuel situation and advised the pilot he was flying in the slipstream of the lead plane and using a lot of fuel. Waisath suggested the pilot drop down a few feet to conserve fuel, but Boehme was determined to maintain his place in the formation, flying very close to the lead plane. Culver could clearly see the tail gunner in the plane in front of them. Just a few feet separated the nose of his plane from the tail of the lead plane.

They reached the primary target, Linz, and began the bomb run. Both the Initial Point and the target were completely obscured and faulty radar equipment on the lead plane made it impossible to bomb the target. The group turned and began a second bomb run on the alternate target, the Neudorf Aircraft Engine Factory, at Graz. They had used a lot of fuel by now. This time the group dropped their bombs over the clouded target. The 460th had bombed the target a few minutes before them and the resulting smoke obscured the factory.[2] They were in flak for a couple of minutes, but Culver's plane wasn't damaged.

As they came off bomb run, Waisath checked the fuel gauges again and told Boehme they didn't have enough fuel to make it back to Italy. They left the formation over Lake Balaton, in Hungary and the pilot began calling BIG FENCE.[3] **(Author's note: BIG FENCE was the call sign for a VHF radio station, used in emergencies, primarily by damaged planes and planes low on fuel in need of assistance. By providing a test count, BIG FENCE operators could home in on the radio signal of the aircraft, identifying the plane's position and provide a "steer" to the nearest friendly base or the closest friendly territory.)** The bombardier, Weintritt, ordered the crew to lighten the aircraft by jettisoning all unnecessary equipment overboard. To further complicate matters, they flew over some more flak batteries and were peppered by shrapnel from the exploding shells. Fortunately, no one was injured. Two engines were damaged, but the plane was able to continue.[4]

It was soon apparent they weren't going to make it to a friendly landing field. Their fuel situation was critical. Boehme put out a MAYDAY call. Culver didn't wait any longer. He headed to the bomb bay and saw the radio operator, Goldman, at the entrance. He told Goldman to jump as soon as he heard the bail out bell. The bell sounded and Goldman didn't move. Culver didn't hesitate. He pushed Goldman out of the plane into the slipstream and jumped himself.[5] They were just off the coast of Yugoslavia, north of Zara.

Culver pulled the ripcord and the chute opened with a jolt. It was déjà vu, but this time with a slight difference. He was glad his uniform wasn't drenched with gasoline, as it had been on his first bail out, but there was another immediate worry. Culver heard "pfft" sounds near him and above him, in his parachute. He quickly realized the sounds were bullets, passing nearby. He was a sitting duck, but there wasn't much he could do about it. Culver looked down and saw he was in the middle of a bay, about a mile offshore. He didn't notice any more parachutes as he descended. Culver looked toward shore, but was too far away to see who was shooting at him. When he got closer to the water, he heard the shots coming from one side of the bay and saw a very welcome sight, a British Spitfire fighter plane, coming in low over the shoreline. To his relief, the fighter made a strafing run along the coast, temporarily suppressing the fire. The Spitfire pilot saluted Culver as the plane pulled up from its strafing run and Culver waved back. The Spitfire flew off. Culver realized the pilot must have heard Boehme's distress call from minutes earlier.

As Culver drifted over the bay he could hear someone calling for help in the water. He didn't see anyone and there wasn't much he could do. The water was coming up quickly. He didn't want to get tangled up in the parachute or its lines. When he was about 50 feet above the water he unbuckled the straps on his parachute harness and plunged into the water. It was a long distance to fall, but he was determined to get away from that parachute.

As soon as he surfaced, Culver started swimming toward the shore on the opposite side of the bay from where he heard the shots. Fortunately, he was a strong swimmer. He was at least a mile from shore, so he began swimming the breast stroke. In this way, he was able to present the smallest target to the shooters. His Mae West life preserver helped keep him afloat.

Bishop followed Culver out the bomb bay. Weintritt, Brown, Lohr and Oliver bailed out the camera/escape hatch in the rear of the plane. Jacobson and Boehme were the last to bail out, going through the bomb bay.[6] Some saw the plane crash into the Adriatic, but Culver lost sight of the bomber after he bailed out.

Goldman, Lohr, Brown and Weintritt were captured by the Germans. Waisath, Jacobson, and Oliver were later reported killed in action.[7] It's unknown whether they drowned after parachuting into the water or were killed by enemy fire while in their parachutes.

Twenty-year-old Marija Glavan saw the plane as it flew overhead.[8] Marija belonged to the local resistance movement in her village, called SKOJ (Savez Komunista Omladine Jugoslavije). She was near the beach when she saw the bomber fly out over the bay. Marija lived in the village of Privlaka, near the north end of the bay. She saw objects coming from the plane. They looked like "umbrellas" to her and she soon realized there were men attached to the umbrellas. She heard shooting come both sides of the bay and from her village. The shooting frightened her and she ran into a field and hid behind a wall.

As she looked out into the bay, Marija saw two men in the water. One was closer to the shore, but both were far from land. She waited and watched until the closest swimmer finally approached. The tired and wet airman pulled himself out of the water and ran inland from the beach. Marija followed at a distance and watched him run into a vineyard.

45. Marija Glavan

Marija ran to her home. She picked up some clothes and ran back to the vineyard, where she found the airman hiding behind some bushes. She didn't know his name, but she had found Bishop. He looked scared and very young. He was wearing his wet flying suit and she handed him the clothes she brought from the house. They were her clothes. Bishop understood and began putting them on, assisted by Marija. Despite the circumstances, Bishop couldn't resist a smile as he donned the women's clothes.

It was not safe to stay there. Although they couldn't see any Germans, Marija knew they would soon be searching the area. Now there was constant gunfire. The Germans had set up a machinegun in the church tower, out of Marija's view and they were firing at something or someone in the area. They started running away from the sounds of gunfire, Bishop following Marija. She pointed in a direction for him to run. She stopped running, but motioned for Bishop to keep going. Bishop left in the direction pointed out by Marija and was soon picked up by another group of villagers, who took him to a cellar and gave him mens clothing.

Meanwhile, Culver made his way to shore, exhausted after a two-hour swim. A young woman met him on the beach and took him to a nearby outbuilding. Another woman gave him a glass of clear liquid. He was thirsty and took several gulps, at first not realizing it was some sort of alcohol. It burned his throat, but quickly warmed him and he began to feel better. The women left him alone.

In a short while a man arrived and took him to a house, gave Culver dry clothes to replace his wet flying suit and left. He didn't speak English, but Culver assumed he should wait in the house.

Culver was alarmed to see that his next visitors were German soldiers. They searched him for weapons and papers, removed his dog tags and then took him to a stockade. On arrival, he was interrogated by a German lieutenant with a swagger stick. Culver provided his name, rank and serial number. The German spoke excellent English and began asking him other questions, more specifics about his group and mission. Culver refused to answer. The German hit him a glancing blow on the shoulder with the swagger stick, but didn't pursue the matter further and dismissed Culver.

German guards took Culver back to the stockade. There were several other men in the compound. He didn't pay any attention to them, didn't recognize any of them as being from his crew and didn't try to communicate with anyone. He was more concerned about his own situation. He couldn't tell if any were Americans.

Later in the evening Culver heard gunfire outside the compound. He didn't know who was shooting, but there was a lot of noise. The door to his cell suddenly opened. He walked to the door and saw a German soldier just outside. He hit the German a hard blow and then took off into the darkness, not looking back. Culver ran from the building and into the darkness, amidst the gunfire. He kept a low profile and ran full speed away from the compound. After he had run quite some distance from the building and away from the gunfire, he stopped to catch his breath and hid in some bushes. Within a few minutes a young woman found him. She tugged on his clothes, beckoning him to follow her. It was Marija Glavan, accompanied by her cousin, Anka Glavan.

Both girls were pulling at him, talking in their language and motioning for him to follow. With Marija leading the way, they ran to a vineyard. Anka followed, dragging branches to hide their footprints. Marija motioned for Culver to get into a hole in the ground. She grabbed him and pushed him into the hole. Culver couldn't see in the darkness, but got in the hole. The girls hurriedly covered the hole with some boards. Culver heard the sound of dirt being piled on the boards. Soon it was quiet. Marija and Anka left.

The girls returned to their homes. The Germans seemed to be everywhere in the village. They were going house to house, searching for the missing airmen. Marija lived with her mother and the Germans soon arrived. The Germans came into the house, demanding to know where the Americans were. One yelled, "Wo ist Americanen? Wo ist Partizanen?" Both women were terrified and Marija's mother was crying, but neither said anything. Apparently satisfied, the soldiers left.

About an hour later Culver heard the voices speaking German. The voices got louder as they approached and he heard their dogs barking. It was a German patrol searching for him. At the same time he felt a critter of some sort crawling on his lower body. He thought it was a rat, but he had no room to move and didn't dare to try, for fear of attracting the soldiers. After what seemed like an eternity, it was quiet again. The Germans and their dogs hadn't found him. It wasn't long before other local resistance members arrived. They uncovered the hole and took him to where he left his wet clothing. He retrieved some personal items from the gear.

These civilians briefly stopped with Culver at the home of Jakov Zoric, a member of the resistance, and moved out into the night, avoiding German patrols that were searching for the downed airmen. They finally returned to the shore, found a rowboat and rowed to the nearby island of Vir. They spent the remainder of the night there. The next morning they went to another nearby island, Molat, where they spent the day and night.

The next morning a British PT boat arrived. By this time Bishop had joined Culver, having taken the same route. As Culver boarded the boat, he was stopped by a British seaman who wasn't going to allow him aboard. In peasant clothes Culver didn't look much like a rescued American airman. The situation quickly changed when Culver started talking, with his noticeable Oklahoma accent. Culver was welcomed aboard the boat and they were taken to the island of Vis, where they spent the night. The next day a C-47 flew Bishop and Culver to Bari, Italy.

Boehme returned to Italy three days later. He also parachuted in the water, a few miles from where Boehme and Bishop landed. Boehme started swimming to shore and floundered, caught up in the parachute lines. Fortunately for Boehme, Nikica Peros and his cousin Niko saw several parachutes coming out of the B-24 as it came from the north. Both were part of the local resistance movement in their village, called the "Narodno Oslobodilacki Otpor". Germans in the area fired at the men in the parachutes, with rifles, machineguns and light anti-aircraft weapons. Most of the firing was coming from the north side of Zaton Bay, near the village of Klanice. At least one of the airmen was hit while in his parachute.

46. Niko Peros   47. Nikica Peros

The Peros cousins saw Boehme struggling in the water, caught up in the parachute lines. Niko, a strong swimmer, was first in the water, followed by Nikica, who had a knife. They swam out to Boehme and Nikica cut Boehme free from the parachute lines and both helped him to shore. As they swam to shore, the Germans started shooting at them with machineguns. The Germans were less than a mile away, so the three men got out of the immediate area as quickly as possible, running away from the main concentration of German troops.

They took Boehme to the village of Zaton. The villagers gave him civilian clothes and hid him from the Germans, who were searching the entire area for missing flyers. The Germans suspected villagers in Zaton were hiding the airman and gave them an ultimatum of turning over the airman or facing the consequences. The villagers refused to betray Boehme, so the Germans shelled the village, ultimately killing a young girl in the barrage. The Germans then scoured the village, looting as they searched the houses. The searching and looting continued for four days.

Three other members of the local resistance, Sime Patrk, Jalenka Stulic and Pave Stulic arrived to get Boehme and they left Zaton on foot, managing to stay away from the German patrols. They walked and hid, traveling north from Zara, but staying near the coastline. They eventually took Boehme to some islands off the coast and arranged his evacuation to Vis. From there he returned to Italy on October 22nd. Both Niko and Nikica joined the Partisans after this. Sadly, Niko was killed in an ambush by the Ustashe just weeks before the war ended.[9]

Culver was offered the opportunity to remain in Italy, providing lectures and training to other airmen about Escape and Evasion. Along with this offer came a promotion to Warrant Officer. He considered the offer, but ultimately rejected it. He just wanted to go home. He had already spent more time on the ground, evading the Germans, than he had spent in the air, on combat missions. Since he had been a POW, he was taken off flying status. He opted to return to the U.S. and went to Naples to wait for a boat to take him home. Culver arrived back in the U.S. shortly before Christmas.

Boehme continued flying combat missions. He went down again on November 17th, returning from Blechhammer and managed to make it out of Yugoslavia safely. On that occasion he was found and rescued by the Chetniks. After finding himself in the midst of a battle between the Chetniks and the Partisans, the Chetniks eventually turned Boehme over to the Partisans, who arranged for his safe return to Italy a month later. [10]Boehme was ultimately killed on February 16, 1945, while flying with the group commander, Colonel John Tomhave, when the plane was shot down by flak returning from a mission to Regensburg.

✪ The Story ✪

It was 9 o'clock in the evening in a village along the Dalmatian coast of Croatia when 81 year-old Marija Skoblar heard the knock on the door as she and her husband relaxed on their porch. She looked out and saw a young stranger, standing there. He asked if he could come in. She answered, "Yes, of course," and invited him in. She asked how she could help him. His next words shocked her. The stranger, Sime Lisica, said she had greetings from America. She asked "From whom?" He paused and answered "From Bill Culver, a flyer you rescued in 1944."

There was a brief silence in the room as Marija sat, stunned. She looked at her husband and began sobbing. Her next words, directed to her husband were "Didn't I tell you! Didn't I tell you!" Her sobbing continued as she sat there.

When she regained her composure, Marija explained to the young man that she had never forgotten the two American airmen she rescued near her village. In fact, just a few days before his arrival she talked to her husband and son about the two flyers, wondering if they made it back to Italy safely, wondering if they survived the war and wanting to know who they were. She had so many questions. She could never forget these Americans. Her husband nodded in agreement. Like her, they were so young! She wondered aloud if she could somehow identify them, if she could find them. Her son and husband both encouraged her to forget about the flyers. It had been too long. It was impossible to find these answers. In her heart she couldn't forget. She vowed to both, "You will see that one day before I die I will find them, somehow."

Sime produced the photo of the American bomber crew, as well as the individual photo of Bill Culver. Marija clutched the photos, still sobbing, and kissed both photos. She recognized Bob Bishop in the crew photo, remembering how he had smiled, despite the dangerous situation. She also recognized Bill Culver in the other photo, describing him as the airman she had pushed into the hole and covered. She looked up at Sime and said, "Please try to understand how I feel." Then she began her story.

Sime Lisica grew up hearing the story about the bomber that flew over his village, spilling men and parachutes as it flew out over the bay. He never forgot the story and wanted to learn more about the men and plane as he grew older. Villagers talked about it, how some of the men died and how some were captured. Now a 25 year-old college student in Zagreb, he continued his search for information.

Lisica found a group of local divers, sympathetic to his cause. From local witnesses they knew approximately where the plane went down and eventually located parts of it in 140 feet of water. Luckily, they found part of the tail with the aircraft number still visible. This would help him in his search and he made an inquiry on a website.

Meanwhile, I was writing the first draft of this story. I met Bill Culver a couple of years ago at a reunion of the 485th Bomb Group. Based on my initial research I thought he died when his plane went down. When I explained to him that I thought he was dead he commented that he felt pretty good for a dead man.

This certainly wasn't the first time I was mistaken. He told me of his brief stint as a POW and agreed to talk with me later. Bill and I had subsequent phone conversations and exchanged letters. I searched for others on that crew, but couldn't find any of them still living. I found evidence that Bishop died a few years ago. Armed with debriefing statements from Bishop and Culver, made shortly after their return to Italy and my interviews with Culver, I wrote my first draft of this story. I found it brief and incomplete.

As I reviewed my draft I decided to talk to Culver again. I phoned him and got additional details, but I still wasn't satisfied.

I wondered if the plane had gone down over the bay or if it had crashed on one of the many islands in the region. I wondered about the people who rescued Culver. I had no contacts in Croatia and no means to pursue this further.

Then I was contacted by a friend in North Carolina, Laura Sharpe, who knew of my background and research. Laura saw a posting on a website, requesting information on a B-24 bomber that was found in Croatia. She asked if I might have a means of identifying the plane from my records. A lot of B-24s, B-17s and other Allied bombers went down in different regions of Yugoslavia during WWII. I knew of at least 25 or 30 planes from the 485th Bomb Group alone that went down there, many of them in the water. As busy as I was at the time, I agreed to check my records for a B-24 with a tail number of 42-51559.

The answer sent a shudder up my spine. This was the same plane and crew I was writing about! It just couldn't be. With all the planes and all the stories, well, it just couldn't be. Yet it was. Sometimes I've learned that it's better to just accept these things and appreciate them. I contacted Sime Lisica immediately, still not believing my good fortune. I was still skeptical, until I received the photos with the tail numbers visible. One again the story gods smiled down on me.

I shared my research information and crew photos with Sime, requesting that he attempt to identify the local villagers who helped the three airmen. I wouldn't have had to ask, since he wanted answers just as much as I did. Through his tenacious efforts, we now have answers.

More importantly, Marija Skoblar and Bill Culver have answers. Despite having some health concerns, Bill recently told me he and his wife might just make a trip to Croatia to meet this woman who rescued him. That would make a perfect ending to this story.

JW

48. Diver approaches wreckage

49. Tail of B-24 with serial number visible

50. Sime Lisica, Croatian researcher

NOTES AND REFERENCES

1 From *We Remember Mission #58 August 10, 1944*, written by the crew of Miss Fitz (2004) and Escape Statement

[2] 485th Bomb Group mission report for 10/16/44

[3] Reference to call for BIG FENCE from 485th Bomb Group mission report for 10/16/44

[4] Reference to damaged engines from Lt. Boehme's Evasion Form, completed 10/23/44, 15th AAF archives

[5] Culver's personal account is from his Evasion Form, dated 10/20/44, 15th AF archives. Additional info was obtained from his unpublished memoirs and from phone interviews with the author on 3/18/05 and 6/11/05.

[6] Order of bailout and bailout locations from letter Kenneth Lohr wrote to USAAF at the end of WWII, while requesting additional info about the crew. From MACR 9196.

[7] From MACR 9196

[8] Marija Skoblar, nee Marija Glavan provided the details of her rescue of Bishop and Culver to Sime Lisica in an interview on 6/21/05. A few details don't match Culver's 1944 statement and more recent info obtained from him, but one must remember that 60 years have elapsed. There is no doubt that Marija rescued both airmen. When some of the specific details

weren't consistent, the author chose to go with Culver's information, since some of the documentation was made by Culver immediately after he returned, when details were fresh in his mind.

[9] Nikica Peros, one of Boehme's rescuers, provided the details of Boehme's evasion in an interview with Sime Lisica, in early May 2005.

[10] From Richard Boehme's Escape Statement, dated 12/16/44 15th AF archives.

Alternate Target

An event occurred on February 23, 1945, which would be memorialized forever in American history. As American Marines continued to suffer heavy casualties, several Marines and one Navy Corpsman raised the American flag on Mt. Suribachi on the island of Iwo Jima. This event was captured on camera by photographer Joe Rosenthal and later sculpted into the famous monument at Arlington National Cemetery. This date was also imprinted on the memories of some of the Boys from Venosa. There would be no monument for them, unless one counts the crosses representing those who were lost that day.

The mission was part of Operation CLARION, a two day maximum effort for the U.S. Air Force and the Royal Air Force, targeting Axis railroads and communications targets throughout occupied Europe. Fancy code names didn't impress those who were flying. If they were impressed with anything, it was the fact that one more mission completed meant one mission less to fly and one step closer to their return home. Their target for the day was the Wels marshaling yard in Austria. If bad weather clouded the target, the first alternate target was the marshaling yard at Bruck, Austria. There would be no complaints if they had to bomb the alternate, since intelligence reports indicated there were only six flak guns in the vicinity of Bruck.

One of the Boys preparing for the mission was 2nd Lt. Bill Ryan from the 828th Bomb Squadron. Ryan was the copilot on 1st Lt. John Hazel's crew. They had been at Venosa for six months and Ryan was no stranger to combat, having flown 13 sorties. Ryan had grown up on his own. His mother died when he was three years old and he hadn't seen his dad since he was ten. After spending time with various people in different places, he was taken in by a foster family. He graduated from high school in Phoenix, Arizona and was lucky enough to get into the Air Force. He turned 20 before going overseas.

51. Lt. Robert Ware's crew, 828th B.S. Back row, left to right: Henry Ring, waist gunner; William Sniegowski, top turret; Ed Hope, nose gunner; Stephen Parise, radio operator; Jack Yates, tail gunner, and James Lazarakis, ball gunner. Front row, left to right: Jack Hubbard, navigator; Arthur Daehn, bombardier; Jack Whatley, copilot and Robert Ware, pilot. Parise and Whatley were not on the Bruck mission.

On this day Ryan was flying with the crew of 1st Lt. Robert Ware. Ware's copilot, 2nd Lt. Jack Whatley, had an eye infection and was grounded by the flight surgeon. Ware's crew had five missions to their credit. The Operations Officer for the 828th Squadron would be flying with Hazel's crew, replacing Ryan, leading "B" Box in the formation. Ryan noted at briefing that he'd be flying directly behind his own crew, in the #4 position, known as "the slot".

52. Bill Ryan in front of his tent

There was a reason for their formation position. Ware's crew had "Panther" in their plane. Panther was a secret radar-jamming device, recently added to some of the 485th's inventory to give them a better chance of survival against the German radar-controlled flak batteries. Planes equipped with this tool were normally positioned in the center of each box, in order to offer the most protection for the group. A newly-trained Panther operator was also flying with Ware's crew. Tom Tabor, the senior Panther operator in the squadron, was originally assigned to fly in Ware's plane that day. Merl Shields, the red-headed radio operator from 1st Lt. August Horvath's crew, replaced Tabor and Tabor flew with another crew. Shields' station in the aircraft during the bomb run was at a table directly behind the copilot, where there was radar-jamming equipment in addition to various radios that normally occupied this station. Shields was anxious to practice his skills on Panther. Ryan didn't know Ware or anyone else on the crew, but had seen some of them around the base.

Ryan was trying something different today.[1] A few days prior, he had been assigned the duties of Personal Equipment Officer on a day he wasn't flying. It was his duty to make sure the crews flying that day had their necessary gear and to assist with any last minute equipment needs. He noticed a few of the pilots were wearing back parachutes. Ryan, like many other pilots, still wore the chest parachute, commonly called the chest pack. He put his chute behind his seat on missions. If he had to bail out, it was a simple matter to grab the parachute and clip it to

53. Merl Shields

the front of his harness. But it still took a few seconds. He knew these few seconds might be critical in an emergency. He talked to the supply sergeant in the equipment shack about getting one of the back chutes. The supply sergeant measured him for the harness and said it would take a few days to prepare it. The harness was now ready, so he would be wearing the back parachute today for the first time.

1st Lt. Clarence Adams was another pilot preparing for this mission. He and his 830th Squadron crew would be flying in the slot position in "A" Box of the formation. It would be a memorable day for them.

54. Lt. C.D. Adams crew, 830ᵗʰ B.S.. Back row, left to right: John Sellers, navigator/bombardier; Morris Rabinovitz, copilot; Claude Smith, radio operator/waist gunner; James McGinley, top turret, and Willie Bates, tail gunner. Front row, left to right: Van Anagnost, ball gunner; C.D. Adams, pilot; Bernard Reagan, nose gunner, and Lemar Sharpe, engineer/waist gunner. This photo was taken on the flight line on the day the crew was shot down.

Twenty eight planes from the 485ᵗʰ took off for their target in Austria. They formed into four boxes, seven planes in each box and joined up with the 460ᵗʰ Bomb Group. Three of the planes turned back with mechanical problems and the rest of the group headed north to Austria. The 460th led the mission and pulled away from the 485ᵗʰ. Soon the 460ᵗʰ commander radioed the 485ᵗʰ, advising the primary target was undercast. At this point the 485ᵗʰ commander changed course, heading for the first alternate target, the marshaling yard at Bruck.

Before long, the 485ᵗʰ was approaching Bruck. The lead bombardier was unable to identify the target on the first pass. The group followed the lead bomber as it made a wide turn and approached the target again! This time, for reasons unknown, "A"

Box pulled out to one side, leaving "B" Box in the lead. So far there had been no flak. Hazel's bombardier, 2nd Lt. Al Trinche, was now the lead bombardier. He dropped his bombs and the rest of the box dropped their load when they saw the first bombs fall from Hazel's plane. The German gunners had plenty of time to find the correct altitude, even without the aid of radar-controlled sights on their 88 millimeter flak guns. The B-24s were flying at 21,000 feet and the flak guns were situated high in the mountains. The bombers were sitting ducks.

To make matters worse, "B" Box leader continued on a straight and true course after the bombs were dropped instead of taking the box into a diving turn. This evasive action was normally taken to throw off the German gunners on their altitude calculations and to get the planes out of the radar range as quickly as possible.

Below, the air raid sirens sounded at Bruck, warning of the approaching American bombers. The villagers ran for shelters and basements. In the local hospital, Laura Fuerst was in labor. Other patients were being evacuated to the bomb shelter but, due to her situation, she couldn't join them. The bombs fell nearby and she could hear the anti-aircraft guns respond. She couldn't help but wonder if the American airmen were as terrified as she was, lying there helpless and feeling the concussions from the explosions.[2]

Shortly after the bombs were dropped, flak started bursting within the formation. The flak seemed to be coming up in bursts of five. The first burst was in front of Hazel's lead plane, at the same altitude. The second shell burst under the right wing of Hazel's plane, lifting the wing dramatically, nearly flipping the bomber over. The third burst was under the tail of the Hazel's bomber and the concussion raised the tail several feet. The fourth burst was in the nose of Ware's plane and the fifth shell went into its bomb bay.[3]

Ryan felt like he was in an elevator going up when the plane was first hit in the nose. The first burst may have killed the nose gunner, S/Sgt Ed Hope and bombardier, 2nd Lt. Art Daehn. The first concussion was followed almost immediately by a "pranging" sound, the sound of metal piercing metal as a second shell passed through the bomb bay, but didn't explode.

Ryan knew they were in serious trouble. He yelled to Ware over the intercom that they'd better get out. The plane had gone into a dive to the left. Ryan looked over to see Ware slumped over the controls, unconscious. Ryan reacted quickly, unbuckling his safety harness. Gravity pulled him to a standing position against the instrument panel. He fought the forces, pulling Ware off the controls at the same time. All his effort was directed at keeping the stricken bomber from colliding with other bombers in the formation. He pulled back on the yoke, at the same time turning hard right and stood on the right rudder, trying to maneuver the plane to the right.

Ryan glanced behind him and saw a gunner with a fire extinguisher making a futile attempt to extinguish the flames coming onto the flight deck from the bomb bay. The plane wasn't responding as Ryan fought the controls, trying to buy precious time for the crew to get out. As flames engulfed the flight deck, he resigned himself to the fact that he wouldn't get out of the burning plane. His exit was blocked by fire. He recalls wondering what his family would think and how they would accept the news.

Boys in other planes watched in horror as the stricken ship pulled out of the formation. Sgt. Tom Tabor, looking out the right the waist window in a plane behind Ware's, was taking photos with a 35 mm camera and took a couple of pictures of the stricken bomber.[4] He saw the copilot pull the pilot off the controls and then calmly sit down, as parachutes blossomed out of the plane. He could see the top hatch, near the top turret, was open. An airman climbed through the hatch and jumped, his chest pack on fire. Tabor could see fire in the waist of the plane and saw the two waist gunners were on fire. It was a terrible sight. Tabor was still looking through the camera viewfinder when the ship blew up and disappeared.

2nd Lt. Joe Russell was flying as copilot in Lt. Horvath's plane, in the #5 position, slightly behind and to the right of Ware's plane. Just after they dropped their bombs, Russell looked to his left and saw Ware's plane take a direct hit near the front of the bomb bay.[5] He saw a flared hole where the unexploded 88 millimeter shell exited the fuselage above the bomb bay and could see the bomb bay doors were still open. A narrow band of fire encircled the plane and the fire was cutting through the fuselage, like a torch, just behind the wing. Flames were shooting out the hole in the top of the plane. Russell lost sight of the doomed bomber as it slipped beneath the formation. Gunners in the back of Russell's plane were able to keep the stricken bomber in sight. One saw the plane break into two pieces and the tail lazily floated toward the ground. A waist gunner saw Shields, the radio operator, get out safely. The gunner recognized him as he bailed out safely through the bomb bay by his long red, curly hair. Shields was from their crew.

2nd Lt. Bob Anderson was the bombardier in Horvath's plane. He was standing between the pilots when he looked to the left and saw Ware's plane on fire.[6] They were close enough that he could see the copilot stand up, appear to look around and sit back down. A couple of parachutes came out of the bomb bay. One of the gunners saw Shields bail out. Anderson watched as the nose of the plane separated from the rest of the aircraft in front of the wings. He didn't hear an explosion when the plane broke in half. It was a horrible sight.

Sgt. Henry Ring was at a waist gun when the flak burst hit. Flames leaped into the back of the plane and Ring's arms and face were burned. Cpl. James Lazarakis extracted himself from the ball turret and retreated through the flames to the back of the plane with Ring. Cpl. Robert "Jack" Yates in the tail turret turned around and saw flames engulfing the waist of the plane. He quickly exited the tail and moved to the camera hatch, opening it.

Lazarakis was first to leap through the camera hatch. Ring looked down and saw Lazarakis' parachute pop open, followed by a horrible sight. Lazarakis slipped through the harness and fell to his death. He hadn't attached the leg straps on the parachute harness before jumping. Ring dived through the hatch, followed by Yates.

Ring helped Cpl. Robert Yates, the tail gunner, out the camera hatch and then helped Shields get out. Ring was the last to bail out from the rear of the plane, his arms badly burned from the flames.[7]

The top turret gunner, Sergeant William Sniegowski, made it to the bomb bay. He saw the navigator, Flight Officer Jack Hubbard, at the back of the flight deck. Sniegowski motioned for Hubbard to leave, but Hubbard didn't move. Sniegowski bailed out.

Al Trinche later wrote to Ryan's foster parents, providing them with information.

24 March 1945

Dear Mr. And Mrs. Ridgeway[8]:

I am the bombardier on the crew your son, William T. Ryan 0-776066 is on. I realize how you must feel, since I know how my own people felt when I went down in Yugoslavia with our navigator on 18 December. No doubt Bill wrote to you about this and I believe my wife also wrote to you for any information you might have.

First of all, let me say that I firmly believe that Bill has a good chance of getting back, although it may take quite a while. One of the fellows we came back from Yugoslavia with had been missing in action since last July!![9]

Our tail gunner called out that Bill's ship had been hit. Hutch (our navigator) and I looked out of the nose windows and by that time the ship had slid off to the right and we could see what happened from then on. Just as we looked out, the plane had broken in half at the bomb bays and it started going down in a flat spin with all four engines running. There was a little fire from the bomb bays, but not very much. All the chutes we could count were seven, before we lost sight of the plane, and it seemed that the plane had quite a way to go before striking the ground-so it is entirely possible that the remaining chutes had time to open. When the plane was hit, a pilot flying off Bill's wing saw him rise from his seat and then sit down again. So we can see that he was not injured by the flak. He also wore a back type parachute and not the detachable chest type, as most of us wear. All he had to do was get out of the plane without bothering to snap on a chest type chute. He had plenty of altitude in his favor, which makes me hopeful that he was able to get to the bomb bays, which were open at the time and only about eight feet behind him, and get out.

That is all there is to tell and I do wish you to have all the hope and confidence that Bill will be heard from sooner or later. Hutch and I feel very hopeful about the matter and I don't feel that we are hoping in vain. I realize how terrible these past few weeks must be for you, but I can't urge you enough to have confidence and not lose hope for Bill's eventual return. I pray that it will be soon.

Sincerely,
Albert Trinche

Suddenly, Ryan wasn't flying the plane anymore. The plane had exploded and he was blown out. His last recollection was of hearing a dull roar and then he lost consciousness. He felt himself falling through the air and saw the ground several thousand feet below him. He came to his senses, realized what happened and pulled the ripcord on his new back parachute. He kept pulling on the ripcord until he looked up and saw the canopy. He estimated he was at 8,000 feet when the parachute opened.

He took stock of his condition. He had cuts on his head. When he looked down, he saw the cloth on the left leg of his flight suit was missing. He felt severe pain in his left leg. He saw that all the flesh was missing between his left knee and hip and he could see his leg bone.

Ryan was in a mountainous area and worried about landing on his wounded leg. He had heard that the direction of descent could be controlled by manipulating the lines on the parachute. Below him and off to one side was a river. He thought he might be able to change direction and land in the river, a soft alternative to the rugged slopes. When he tried to manipulate the shroud lines, air began to spill from the parachute, increasing the rate of descent. Realizing this wasn't a good idea, he wisely decided to let the parachute follow its own course.

Ryan saw that some of the panels on the parachute were ripped, but couldn't do anything about it. As he drifted down, he heard pieces of his bomber striking the ground. He could also hear dogs barking. He landed in some trees on a steep slope and the parachute caught in the treetops, the branches slowing his fall to earth.

He disconnected the parachute and began to slide down the mountain, until a sapling stopped him. Here on the side of the mountain he took stock of his condition. He had a head wound that was bleeding profusely. His leg was in bad shape. The front of his body showed imprint lines from all the wires of his heated flying suit. To cause these injuries, he realized he must have been blown through the windshield, an opening less than 12 inches in height.

Ryan knew he was seriously injured and couldn't walk, so he had no option but to wait and hope someone would find him. It was rugged, mountainous area and he saw no sign of life around him. He hoped some of the others made it out of the plane safely, but he hadn't seen any of them.

As the remainder of the bomber force left the target area, 1st Lt. Clarence Adams' plane was in serious trouble. Adams saw Ware's plane blow up over the target area but he had problems of his own. His plane was hit by a flak burst and the ailerons and hydraulics were shot out. The plane went into a dive and fell about 10,000 feet as Adams struggled with the controls. He finally gained control at 10,000 feet by jockeying the engine throttles. He realized he couldn't make it back to Italy with the throttles as his only means of controlling the plane. He asked the navigator for a heading to the nearest friendly territory. The navigator, 2nd Lt. John Sellers, plotted a course to Zara, Yugoslavia, where there was reportedly an emergency landing field in Partisan hands.

As the bomber reached Yugoslavia, Adams decided a bailout was safer than risking a landing on a short emergency field without hydraulics and with limited control. Adams had his crew bail out and jumped himself. They were about 30 miles from Zara. Adams saw several others below him in their parachutes. He watched them land and saw trucks coming to pick them up. He hoped they were Partisans. He saw the ground coming up rapidly, hit and lost consciousness. When he came to, he was bleeding from a head wound and being carried on the back of a big Yugoslav Partisan.

The entire crew was immediately picked up by Partisans. The ball gunner, Sgt. Van Anagnost, seriously injured his back in the bail out and others had minor injuries. Within a few hours, the crew was taken to a landing area and picked up by an American C-47. They were safely back in Italy that evening.[10]

Of the 25 bombers on this mission, two planes didn't return, thirteen bombers received minor damage and two suffered major damage. They had only been in range of the flak gunners for two or three minutes, but the gunners were accurate.

Of the enlisted airmen on Ware's crew that day Ryan, Ring, Shields, Sniegowski and Yates made it safely to the ground. Ring, Shields and Sniegowski were captured almost immediately. Yates was taken by a local farmer to a farmhouse where German soldiers took him into custody.

Ware was also blown out of the aircraft. He was severely wounded, but managed to deploy his parachute. He landed in a tree nursery near Bruck. He was given first aid by a Dr. Olynetz, but died shortly thereafter from his injuries. Ware was buried two days later in the village of Frohnleiten. Local villagers supplied the casket and he was buried by civilians and French POWs.[11]

Shields was severely beaten when he landed and taken to Bruck in a horse cart by his captors. A local Nazi businessman, Hans Reiter, incited some of the locals when Shields arrived, urging them to kill Shields. Lt. Ludensky, an SS Officer, intervened, chastising Reiter and telling him if he wanted to fight he should go to fight the Russians, instead of shooting an unarmed airman who was no threat. Shields was not harmed after this incident.[12]

The four gunners were reunited at the airfield near Linz. They were eventually taken to Frankfurt for interrogation and survived the war as POWs.[13]

Ryan waited on the ground, becoming more concerned about his own situation. He tried to fashion a tourniquet for his wounded leg, but this seemed to make the wound bleed even more. Finally, he just lay there, reflecting on his situation. Evasion would be impossible due to his condition. In the unlikely situation that pro-Allied Austrians or Partisans found him, they would not be able to take him to a hospital. Unfortunately, his only chance for survival was to be captured and taken to a hospital. Being captured was risky, especially if found by civilians who had just been bombed, but he really had no choice in the matter. He had to wait and hope he'd be found by people who wouldn't kill him. Here he was on a mountainside, several miles from Bruck. He was getting cold lying on the snow-covered mountain slope, and the shock was wearing off. He couldn't imagine this was really happening to him.

About two hours later Ryan saw six young men approaching him. Two of them were in uniform, but didn't appear to be regular German army. They were young men and didn't speak

English. They pointed their rifles at him as they approached. He couldn't understand what they said, but they weren't un-friendly. They took his escape kit from him, removed the fifty gold-seal dollars and returned the kit and its remaining contents. Four of the young men left, including the two in uniform.

The remaining two were trying to be helpful. They built a fire so he could warm himself. Ryan didn't know what was going to happen, but it was obvious that they meant him no harm. In a while one of the others returned with a stretcher. The three men loaded him onto the stretcher and started carrying him down the mountain. They were obviously locals and knew the area well.

After a couple of hours they came to a cottage and Ryan was carried inside. There, a middle-aged woman tended a fire in the fireplace and served him hot soup. No words were spoken. Ryan felt better after eating the soup. When he finished, the young men carried him outside and lifted him onto a two-wheeled horse-drawn cart, and they started again down the mountain-side. It was dark when they started out and several hours later they arrived at a town several miles south of Bruck. They took him through the streets and stopped in front of a hospital. The young men carried him inside, placed him on a litter on the floor and left.

While Ryan was on the floor, a German soldier walked up to him and said, "American swine", and walked away. If this was the worst treatment, he could easily handle it. A nurse approached and began asking him questions in English. He provided his name, rank and serial number, but refused to answer any other questions. This would be his first and last interrogation. She wanted to know his group and unit, but she didn't push the issue after he refused to answer. He was carried upstairs to the treatment area, which appeared to be an operating room.

A doctor examined him but didn't give him any medication for his pain. After cleaning the wound, the doctor put a temporary splint on his leg. He showed Ryan an American dog tag and pointed to the "O" on the number, obviously wanting to know what it stood for. Ryan tried to explain that it stood for "Officer". He looked at the dog tag more closely and saw it was Robert Ware's. He told the doctor he wanted to know what happened to Ware. The doctor understood and pointed to the hallway. Ryan asked to see Ware. Medical staff carried him into the hall and he was shown a body, covered by a tarpaulin. He asked that the tarp be removed and the staff pulled it back, revealing a lifeless airman lying on his back with one arm across his face. Ryan assumed it was Ware, but couldn't see the face clearly.

Ryan was carried to a nearby building, not part of this main hospital. There he spent the night, exhausted. The next morning he was very thirsty and hungry, having had nothing to drink or eat except melted snow and the bowl of soup. Ryan got the orderly's attention and mimicked eating motions. The orderly left, returning with a basin of hot water, a razor and a mirror. Ryan obviously hadn't made himself clear, but he used the opportunity to clean up. He was surprised when he looked in the mirror and saw he had a black eye and his face and head were covered with dried blood. He was fed later.

Ryan looked around the room and, from what he saw, decided he was in some kind of a Red Cross building. He wondered what happened to the rest on the crew. Ware was the only one he could account for.

Later a little girl came in. She was allowed to approach him and seemed very curious about this American. He remembered he still had his escape kit and retrieved the candy inside and gave it to her. She seemed happy and excited when she left.

An ambulance later arrived to pick him up. He was carried outside and loaded into the back of the ambulance. He was surprised to see a 13 year-old boy with the attendants. The boy seemed interested in him, but also kept eyeing Ryan's fleece-lined, blood-soaked flying boots near the stretcher. Ryan pointed to the boots, asking the boy if he wanted them. The boy nodded, so Ryan gave him the boots. After all, he wouldn't be needing them anymore. They drove him to Graz.

The ambulance finally stopped in front of a building and Ryan was met inside by a portly man who spoke perfect English. The man said, "You'll be with us a while. The war is over for you." Ryan thought he was a German who spoke good English, but this was actually an English POW who was helping the POW patients at the hospital. Ryan's leg was X-rayed by a woman who was very rough with him, the only time he experienced this sort of treatment. A French doctor examined his leg and put a plaster cast on it, with an opening over the damaged parts.

From here he was taken up to the third floor where he joined three American POWs, two pilots and a gunner. There were also eight or nine British POWs on the same floor. It was here that he would start to recover from his injury. He felt much better being with other Americans. The other floors in this hospital were full of wounded German soldiers. The treatment was more than adequate, considering the state of affairs and confusion in the Third Reich at this stage of the war. Their main source of food was Red Cross parcels.

One of the Americans, a B-17 copilot, had a badly damaged leg. For some reason he refused to let the doctor work on it, despite being coaxed by the other Americans to cooperate. Doctors eventually had to amputate the leg, but the boy died within a few days.

The only dangerous moment came when the Boys from the 485th and from other groups in Italy bombed Graz on March 9th. The bombs missed their target by a couple of miles and Ryan heard bombs exploding outside the hospital. Hospital staff carried him to the sub-basement of the hospital, which was actually a cellar beneath the basement. His bed literally jumped into the air as bombs struck one corner of the hospital. Dust engulfed them from the concussion of the nearby bombs and glass flew as windows shattered. Fortunately, there was no retribution against the POW patients after the incident.

Time passed and Ryan began to feel better. Near the end of April, the patients were told the Russians were approaching and the hospital would be evacuated. The war must be going well for the Allies. The ambulatory patients were first to leave. One day stretcher-bearers arrived and the other patients were loaded onto the stretchers and taken to the train station. On May 6th, the four remaining Americans and eleven British patients were put on a train. Some of the cars had racks for stretchers. The stretchers were filled with the seriously wounded German soldiers from the hospital. They assumed they were heading toward the American sector and they were correct.

The train started out and went just a few miles before it stopped, at Bruck. The patients were taken off the train and those who were ambulatory were allowed to take a hot shower near the station. They ate there and spent the night. By this time Ryan was able to hobble around on makeshift crutches. They were put onboard again and resumed their journey on the slow-moving train, traveling through the mountains.

On May 8th, they were still on the train. The conductor came up to Ryan and said, "Yesterday you were my prisoner. Today I'm your prisoner." This was how Ryan and the others learned of the German surrender. The train stopped at a river that morning. The newly liberated Americans were told the bridge was closed. They were on the wrong side of a river separating the Russian zone from the American zone. Ryan got off the train for a little while. He spotted a pile of confiscated weapons nearby. He examined the weapons and decided to take a German Walter P-38 pistol as a souvenir. He got back on the train and waited, wondering what was going to happen now. He watched out the window, as civilians came up to the river. Several jumped into the river and started swimming across it. They were obviously trying to get to the American zone.

After a delay, an American sergeant came on the train, asking if there were Americans aboard. Ryan answered up, identifying himself. The sergeant said, "We'll get you across, sir", and soon the train started moving again. It was good to see that American soldier. They still didn't know exactly where they were being taken, but things were looking up.

Late that day the train stopped at Badgastein, an Austrian town in the mountains. The injured German soldiers and injured Americans were taken to a resort hotel to convalesce. Ryan was quite the sight and not what one would expect of an American officer and pilot. Someone procured a pair of tennis shorts for him and an English soldier's dress olive drab jacket. He still had a cast on his left leg and on his right leg he wore a German riding boot. He and his fellow former POWs settled in. The hotel was primarily filled with the wounded German soldiers who had been on the train. It was a beautiful resort and he had a private room and good accommodations, but he wondered if he and his buddies had been forgotten. He had no way to contact the American forces that must be nearby.

They were there for two or three weeks and he was getting bored. Time seemed to stand still and Ryan began to wonder if the Americans had forgotten him or if they even knew he was there. One day he heard the sound of a vehicle approaching and looked out the window to see a jeep with two American soldiers from the 101st Airborne Division in it. He yelled out the window to them, getting their attention and told them he was an American. They came in to talk to him. They said they heard rumors of American POWs in the area and were searching for them. The soldiers promised they would send an ambulance to evacuate them.

Time went on and there was still no relief, except for some American C rations that were dropped off. Finally, an American major arrived. Ryan explained what had happened to them and told the major he wanted to go home. The major told Ryan of logistical problems in the sector and promised he'd do his best to get them out soon, but urged Ryan to be patient.

Surprisingly enough, the next day eight ambulances arrived and the Americans were loaded into the ambulances. After riding for an hour or two through the mountains, they reached an American field hospital. A friendly American nurse there apparently didn't think Ryan's "uniform" was befitting an officer of his stature. She provided him with a pair of women's army slacks, which had buttons on the side instead of a zipper in the front. At least now he had pants. There was an airfield near the hospital and Ryan was evacuated by C-47 to Reims, France for a couple of days and was then taken to the airport at Paris. A C-54 transport flew Ryan back to the U.S., where he spent another year and a half in American hospitals, recuperating.

Ryan was never decorated for his efforts to keep the stricken bomber from colliding with other planes in the formation and buying the crew precious time to get out of the plane. He's just happy he had that new parachute strapped to his back that day and, with a twinkle in his eye and a smile on his face, he relates how a whole trainload of German soldiers surrendered to him at the end of World War II. Of the ten men on the plane that day, only Ryan, Shields, Sniegowski, Ring and Yates returned safely to the U.S. at the end of the war.

✪ The Story ✪

I hadn't originally intended to include this story. I remember hearing the story about a B-24 that was on fire over a target and the copilot stood up, pulled the dead pilot off the controls and sat back down in the plane to fly it out of the formation, only to die when his plane blew up on him. I probably heard it while doing another interview sometime in the past, but it was a vivid image and was likely a horrible memory to the witnesses.

I met Bill Ryan last year over the phone. He was interested in my first book and other information I collected. He told me he had been a copilot in the 828th Bomb Squadron and had been a POW. I asked more about his experiences and he told me he was shot down over Bruck. As he described his experience, I realized Bill was the man pictured in the vivid image in my mind. Somehow he had survived! I was able to find other eyewitnesses to the incident who were amazed, like I was, to find him alive. This was another story that had to be told.

A researcher in Austria, Jakob Mayer, was able to locate one of the local witnesses to the bombing that day, Laura Fuerst. She provided her story. I recently told Bill about Laura Fuerst's recollections and of her question regarding whether the American experienced the same fear as she felt, lying in a hospital bed that day with bombs falling in the village around her. Bill and I both know of at least one airman who felt that same fear. Laura has the answer now.

JW

NOTES AND REFERENCES

[1] Ryan's account of this mission and the experiences resulting from it were obtained from interviews with Ryan on 1/21/05 and 6/6205.

[2] Phone interview of Mrs. Fuerst by Dr. Jakob Mayer in early May, 2005.

[3] The description of the first shells exploding in the formation is from a letter, dated 6/19/45, to Bill Ryan. The letter is from 2nd Lt. Billy Hutchison, the navigator in the plane directly in front of Ware's plane.

[4] Tom Tabor's observations were obtained in a phone interview with Tom on 2/12/05, with references to a diary that Tabor kept while overseas.

[5] Russell's story is from phone interviews on 2/10/05 and 2/14/05 and from his mission log.

[6] Anderson's information is from a phone interview on 2/14/05.

[7] The information on Ring's observations came from a phone interview with Jack Whatley on 1/19/05. Whatley met with Henry Ring in 1981 and Ring related his experience at that time. Ring also related the details surrounding Sniegowski's exit.

[8] Excerpts from letter Al Trinche wrote to the Ridgeway family on 3/24/45.

[9] Trinche had bailed out over Yugoslavia in late '44 and made it back to Italy safely weeks later.

[10] This information is from a 7/12/03 interview with Van Anagnost and a 1/05 phone interview with Clarence Adams.

[11] This information is from Ware's Individual Deceased Personnel File (IDPF), obtained from the U.S. Army.

[12] Shields revealed details of his experience in a letter to Joe Russell, dated 4/29/84. The specifics of the incident, with names of the participants, are from Frohnleiten police reports, completed by Inspector Anton Rappold on 8/13/45, translated and provided to the author by Georg Hoffman.

[13] Jack Yates confirmed in a 10/23/06 interview in Columbia, S.C. that the four gunners were together at the end of the war.

Epilogue

For those airmen still at Venosa in April 1945, the end of their war came at the end of the month. This group was the last heavy bomb group to begin flying combat missions out of Italy and was one of the first to fold its tents. They flew their last mission to Linz, Austria, on April 25th and immediately began closing down the base. Within five days most of the men were gone, either transferred to other bomb groups in the 55th Bomb Wing or sent home to re-equip and prepare for the invasion of Japan. Evidence of the base at Venosa quickly disappeared.

Those flyers who were assigned to other bomb groups flew no more combat missions. Some ferried supplies to northern Italy at war's end, but there were no more bombing missions to be flown. Most simply waited for transfer home.

Whatever their destination, they often didn't know what happened to their buddies who went down on combat missions. The group had no way of keeping records of those who were killed, since most of the time they didn't know what happened to the men shot down in enemy territory. Unless they returned, they were simply lost. The group had no knowledge of whether those who went down were POWs or were killed. Only in recent years has some of this information become available.

According to recent research, at least 470 from the 485th Bomb Group were killed overseas. This includes 154 men, many who

55. Lynn Cotterman, 831st B.S. navigator, awaiting transportation and transfer to the 464th Bomb Group on April 29, 1945 after he cleaned out his tent.

were ground personnel, who were lost when their ship was sunk while enroute to Italy. Approximately 250 men became POWs. Additionally, 13 men were captured by the Germans, but managed to escape and return safely to Italy. At least 140 men evaded capture and made it back to Italy.[1] There are no records available to determine just how many men were injured.

These are just the losses from one bomb group, the last to arrive and one of the first to leave. When one considers there were 21 heavy bomb groups in Italy, some having been in combat for nearly two years longer than the 485th, one can better understand the losses suffered by the men in the 15th Air Force in their war against the Axis Powers in Europe.

To an Athlete Dying Young
A.E. Housman

The time you won your town the race
We chaired you through the market place;
Man and boy stood cheering by,
And home we brought you shoulder-high.

To-day, the road all runners come,
Shoulder-high we bring you home,

And set you at your threshold down,
Townsman of a stiller town.

Smart lad, to slip betimes away
From fields where glory does not stay
And early though the laurel grows
It withers quicker than the rose.

Eyes the shady night has shut
Cannot see the record cut,
And silence sounds no worse than cheers
After earth has stopped the ears:

Now you will not swell the rout
Of lads that wore their honours out,
Runners whom renown outran
And the name died before the man.

So set, before its echoes fade,
The fleet foot on the sill of shade,
And hold to the low lintel up
The still-defended challenge cup.

And round the early-laurelled head
Will flock to gaze the strengthless dead
And find unwithered on its curls
The garland briefer than a girl's.

---

[1] This is the number of flyers listed in evasion reports. This figure does not include the large number of airmen who landed at Vis and Zara. Although they had landed in Yugoslavian territory, in most cases they were not reported Missing in Action and no MACR report was completed. If these airmen were included, the author believes the figure listed would likely double.

Appendix A

Munich Mission, June 9, 1944

This mission to Munich turned out to be the costliest mission of the entire war for the 485th Bomb Group. Unlike Lt. McNulty's plane, which limped back to northern Italy before being shot down by a Messerschmitt, three of the four other planes lost were shot down closer to the target. The four planes were all from the 829th Bomb Squadron.

The first planes to go down on the bomb run were likely F/O Bond's and Lt. Cathcart's planes. The group most likely approached Munich from the northeast. Bond's plane was attacked by fighters near Staubing and went down. Seven men bailed out and became POWs. Three men were killed. Those who died were Albert Knott, Clarence Nippes, and William Whorton. Lt. Cathcart's plane was also shot down by fighters and went down with a full bomb load. The tail gunner, Allen McBride was killed, but the others made it safely out of the aircraft and became POWs. They went down near Siegenburg.

F/O Latwaitis's plane was shot down by Messerschmitts near Velden, north of Munich, while on the bomb run. The plane exploded and only three airmen survived: Otis Vinson, Morris Burney and Marion Shelor.

Lt. Hugh White's plane was last of the four to go down. Damaged in a fighter attack, they trailed behind the formation. It was soon apparent they couldn't make it over the mountains and set a course for Switzerland. They flew over Innsbruck and were further damaged by flak, forcing them to abandon their plane. The entire crew bailed out safely and became POWs.

It's unknown if men on other planes that made it back to Italy were wounded or killed. What is known is that fifty airmen from the 485th Bomb Group didn't return to Italy that day. Eighteen were killed, thirty one became prisoners and one (Brittin) was captured, escaped, and eventually returned to Italy. Forty of these men were from the 829th Squadron. On this one mission they lost 22% of their squadron.

56. Lt. Hugh White crew's, 829th B.S. Back row, left to right: Benjamin Thigpen, nose gunner; Ben Thompson, radio operator/waist gunner; Gilbert Lish, ball gunner; John Hawk, tail gunner; James Gillett, engineer/ waist gunner and Lawrence Silva, top turret. Front row, left to right: John Norris, bombardier; Hugh White, pilot; Charles Duecker, copilot, and Charles Field, navigator. Duecker was replaced by Lynn Tipson, the Asst. Operations Officer on the June 9th mission and David Roth replaced John Norris as bombardier that day. The entire crew became POWs.

57. Flight Officer John Bond's crew, 829th B.S. The individual members of this crew, not identified in the photo, are Elliot Altshuler, nose gunner; Roy Anderson, waist gunner; John Bond, pilot; Joseph Duffield, navigator; Albert Homan, copilot; Albert Knott, flight engineer; Clarence Nippes, radio operator; Edward Sawyer, bombardier; Thomas Toot, tail gunner, and William Whorton, ball gunner.

58. Lt. Joe Cathcart's crew, 829th B.S. Back row, left to right: Allen McBride, tail gunner; Dewey Halcomb, ball gunner; Leon Best, nose gunner; Marvin Lindsay, radio operator/waist gunner; Roy Mehrkens, flight engineer/waist gunner, and Irvin Wolf, top turret. Front row, left to right: Donald Roehn, bombardier; Joseph Cathcart, pilot; Slayton McGhee, copilot, and Arthur Carlson, navigator.

Munich Mission, June 9, 1944

59. Flight Officer Jonas Latwaitis's crew, 829th B.S. Back row, left to right: Edward Walz, nose gunner; Otis Vinson, flight engineer/waist gunner; Jack Mizrahi, radio operator/waist gunner; Paul Combs, tail gunner; Simon Ventimiglia, ball gunner, and Edgar Pierce, top turret gunner. Front row, left to right: Marion Shelor, bombardier; Jonas Latwaitis, pilot; Elmer Kohler, copilot, and Morris Burney, navigator. (Unknown ground crewman seated in front)

Appendix B

POWS in Bulgaria

In addition to the loss of Smith/Bobier's crew, another B-24 from the 485th Bomb Group was lost on the June 23, 1944 mission to Giurgiu. This was the plane and crew of Lt. Robert Lynn, 831st Bomb Squadron. The plane was hit by flak on the rally off the target. The nose gunner, Sgt. Francis Meech, was believed to have been killed in the plane. Sgt. Jack Robbins, a waist gunner, safely bailed out but wasn't seen alive after that. The others, several badly wounded, bailed out of the burning aircraft.

Lynn's crew bailed out near the town of Giurgiu along the Danube River. The river forms the border between Romania and Bulgaria. Some of the crew landed in Romania and others in Bulgaria. Those landing in Romania and becoming prisoners there were Flight Officer Jack Hammerburg, Sgt. James Bright and Sgt. Wilbur Mattison. Lt. Luke Terry, Lt. Malachi Reddington, Staff Sergeant George Chaplin and Staff Sergeant Gerald Grady became prisoners in Bulgaria, landing near the city of Ruse. Lt. Lynn never reached the Shumen POW camp. Due to severe injuries, he was kept at a hospital in Romania and evacuated in September after the POWs at Shumen were liberated.

One other crew from the 485th Bomb Group was shot down in Bulgaria, on the June 28, 1944 mission to Bucharest, Romania. The target was the Tital Oil Refinery and oil storage facility. This was the 828th Bomb Squadron crew of Lt. John Crouchley. Their plane was severely damaged in a fighter attack and went down near the small village of Churen, unable to make it to Allied territory. Lt. Crouchley stayed in the plane to allow his crew to safely bail out and was unable to get out of the aircraft before it crashed.

The other nine men on Crouchley's crew became prisoners in Bulgaria. An interesting sidelight to this story is that the remains of one airman were recovered from the aircraft after the plane had burned for at least two days. The locals believed they had recovered the bodies of two airmen and buried the remains. They believed they had buried "John Krachali" and this was a name associated with the gravesite. The remains of Crouchley were never identified or returned to his family. Bulgarian professor/historian Stan Stanev and the author believed the location of the crash site was originally erroneously reported in the heat of battle. Eyewitnesses saw a plane go down near Bucharest, Romania and this is where the military searched for the missing pilot and aircraft after the war. In reality, the plane went down many miles away, as reported by survivors, in Bulgaria. Together, these men researched the available records, comparing American and Bulgarian accounts and eventually pinpointed the crash near Churen. The author provided this information to the Dept. of Defense. The crash site was positively confirmed by our military (assisted by Stan Stanev) from wreckage obtained in a preliminary trip. As yet, there has been no excavation of the crash site for Lt. Crouchley's remains (as of May 2012).

Including Major Smith and his crew, a total of 23 airmen from the 485th Bomb Group became POWs in Bulgaria. All survived.

60. Lt. John Crouchley's crew, 828th B.S. Back row, Left to right: Ralph Perillo, gunner; Thomas Langstaff, tail gunner; Edward Johnson, ball gunner; Eugene LaScotte, nose gunner; Donald Turner, flight engineer and William Van Meer, radio operator. Front row, left to right: John D. Crouchley Jr, pilot; Allen G. Meister, bombardier; Forrest Leveille, navigator and William Hays, copilot.

61. Lt. Robert Lynn's crew, 831st B.S. Back row, left to right: Francis R. Meech, nose gunner; Wilbur S. Mattison, ball gunner; Gerald Grady, top turret; James Bright, tail gunner; Jack Robbins, waist gunner and George Chaplin, waist gunner. Luke Terry, copilot; Jesse Minter, pilot; Charles Buel, bombardier, and Jack Hammerburg, navigator. Minter was replaced by Lynn as pilot after this photo was taken.

62. Lt. Robert Lynn

Photo List and Credits

1. 485th Bomb Group Headquarters . 485th Bomb Group archives
2. Lavatory at Venosa . . . . 485th Bomb Group archives
3. Airmen shaving and washing . . . . Deacon Miller collection
4. 831st Squadron toilet . . . . Whiting family collection
5. Al Trinche . . . . William T. Ryan collection
6. 828th Bomb Squadron living area . 485th Bomb Group archives
7. LIFE during winter . . . . 485th Bomb Group archives
8. American Red Cross at flight line . 485th Bomb Group archives
9. Colonel Cairns at bat . . . . 485th Bomb Group archives
10. McNulty crew . . . . Yolanda Lubanovich Stahl
11. Jack Lindsey . . . . Yolanda Lubanovich Stahl
12. Ed and Yolanda Lubanovich . . . Yolanda Lubanovich Stahl
13. Lubanovich and McNulty
    arcade photos . . . . Yolanda Lubanovich Stahl
14. Eugene Brittin . . . . Yolanda Lubanovich Stahl
15. Umberto and Caterina D'Olivo . . D'Olivo family collection
16. D'Olivo sisters . . . . D'Olivo family collection
17. Yolanda and Ed Lubanovich . . . Yolanda Lubanovich Stahl
18. Bobier crew . . . . Bob Bobier collection
19. Harold Jones . . . . Randy Hannum collection
20. Bobier crew . . . . Randy Hannum collection

45. Maria Glavan . . . . Maria Glavan Skoblar collection

46. Niko Peros . . . . Nikica Peros collection

47. Nikica Peros . . . . Nikica Peros collection

48. Culvers' plane in Adriatic . . . . Marino Kvarantan

49. Tail of Culver's plane . . . . Marino Kvarantan

50. Sime Lisica . . . . Sime Lisica

51. Ware crew . . . . Jack Yates

52. Bill Ryan . . . . William T. Ryan collection

53. Merl Shields . . . . Joe Russell collection

54. C.D. Adams crew . . . . John Sellers collection

55. Lynn Cotterman . . . . Lynn Cotterman collection

56. White crew . . . . 485ᵗʰ Bomb Group archives

57. Bond crew . . . . 485ᵗʰ Bomb Group archives

58. Cathcart crew . . . . 485ᵗʰ Bomb Group archives

59. Latwaitis crew . . . . Shelor family collection

60. Crouchley crew . . . . Mark LaScotte collection

61. Lynn crew . . . . 485ᵗʰ Bomb Group archives

62. Lt. Robert Lynn . . . . 485ᵗʰ Bomb Group archives

Bibliography

Baker, Robert. *Tail Heavy* (a personal memoir). Hickory Corners, Michigan: Private printing.

Birdsall, Steve. *Log of the Liberators.* New York: Doubleday, 1973

Bobier, Bob. *My Final Mission* (a personal memoir). Columbus, Ohio: Private printing.

Canin, Paul. *Some World War II Memoirs* (a personal memoir). Berkeley, California: Private printing, 2000.

Cubbins, William R. *The War of the Cotton Tails: Memoirs of a WWII Bomber Pilot.* Chapel Hill, North Carolina: Algonquin Books, 1989.

Culver, Bill. *Frightening Experiences* (a personal memoir). Norman, Oklahoma: Private printing, 2001.

Daniel, Roy. *My Last Combat Mission-No Ordinary Day.* Bend, Oregon: Maverick Publications Inc, 2000.

Dolim, Abel L. *Yesterday's Dragons: The B-17 Flying Fortress over Europe during WWII.* Newark, California: Communications Concepts, 2001.

Downs, William David Jr. *The Fighting Tigers: The Untold Stories behind the Names on the Ouachita Baptist University WWII Memorial.* Fayetteville, Arkansas: Phoenix International, 2004.

Eamon, Jim and Gail. *By God, We Made It!* (a personal memoir of Vernon O. Christensen). Colorado Springs, Colorado: Private printing, 2002.

Freeman, Roger. *B-24 Liberator at War.* London England: Ian Allan, 1983.

Holway, John B. *Red Tails, Black Wings: The Men of America's Black Air Force.* Las Cruces, New Mexico: Yucca Tree Press, 1997.

Kempffer, Harold J. *As I Remember* (a personal memoir). Apple Valley, Minnesota: Private printing, revised edition 2002.

Lindsay, Franklin. *Beacons in the Night: With the OSS and Tito's Partisans in Wartime Yugoslavia.* Stanford, California: Stanford University Press, 1993.

Lloyd, Alwin T. *Liberator: America's Global Bomber.* Missoula Montana: Pictorial Histories Publishing, 1994.

MacLean, William F. *Mission Log from the "Milk Run" to Freedom* (a personal memoir). Private printing, 2004.

Mauritz, Michael. *The Secret of Anzio Bay: A True Story of an American Fighter Pilot in World War II Italy.* Tarentum, Pennsylvania: Word Association Publishers, 2002.

Miller, Francis Trevelyan. *The Complete History of WWII.* Chicago, Illinois: Readers Service Bureau, 1947.

Muirhead, John. *Those Who Fall: An Unforgettable Chronicle of War in the Air.* New York: Random House, 1986.

Newby, Leroy W. *Target Ploesti, View from a Bombsight.* Novato, California: Presidion, 1983.

Palmer, Charles. *The Shumen Diary* (a personal memoir). Morro Bay, California: Private printing, revised edition 2004.

Porter, Claude L. *Cuckoo Over Vienna*. Traverse City, Michigan: Village Press, 1989.

Rasco, Arthur. *Fifty Missions From Broadway* (a personal memoir). El Paso, Texas: Private printing.

Rosner, Bernat and Tuback, Frederic C. *An Uncommon Friendship*. Berkeley, California: University of California Press,2001.

Rust, Kenn C. *Fifteenth Air Force Story*. Temple City, California: Historical Aviation Album, 1976.

Schnackenberg, Elmer J. Jr. *Off We Go Into the Wild Blue Yonder*.....(a personal memoir). Huntersville, North Carolina: Private printing, 2002.

Schneider, Sammy. *This Is How It Was*. St. Petersburg, Florida: Southern Heritage Press, 1995.

Selhaus, Edi. *Evasion and Repatriation: Slovene Partisans and the Rescued American Airmen in WWII*. Manhattan, Kansas: Sunflower University Press, 1993.

Serwatka, Szymon (Mucha, Michal and Kassak, Peter). *Z Ziemi Wloskiej Do Polskiej*. Poland: Biuro Uslug Komputerowych –Stanislaw Smaga, 2003.

Tenhaken, Mel. *BAIL-OUT!* Manhattan, Kansas: Sunflower University Press, 1990

Tharratt, Robert. *I Want You For the U.S. Army* (a personal memoir). Walnut Creek, California: Private printing.

The crew of Miss Fitz. *We Remember Mission #58: August 10, 1944* (a personal crew memoir). Private printing, 2004.

Vuksic, Velimir. *Tito's Partisans 1941-45*. Oxford, England: Osprey, 2003.

Whiting, Wayne and Jerry. *I'm Off To War, Mother, But I'll Be Back.* Walnut Creek, California: Tarnaby, 2001.

Wiktor, Stefan and Kowalczyk, Tadeusz. *Wspomnienia wojenne z Zygodowic i okolicy z lat 1939-1945 (Wartime memoirs from Zygodowice and its surroundings 1939-1945).* Private printing, 1992

Index

A

Aachen, Germany 45
Adams, Clarence 180-181, 187, 197
Adriatic Sea 20
Afrika Corps 4
Albania 58-59
Aleppo, Syria 66
Altshuler, Elliot 205
Ambler, PA 21
Anagnost, Van 181, 188, 197
Ancona, Italy 33
Anderson, Bob 184, 196
Anderson, Captain 122
Anderson, Roy 205
Ankara, Turkey 64-65
Anklem, Germany 130
Arlington National Cemetery 177
Athens, Greece 149, 159
Augustino, Don 34
Auschwitz (Oswiecim) 99-100, 114, 118, 128, 137, 140, 143
Austria 18

B

Badgastein 194
Badoglio, Marshal 4-5, 7, 21
Baldridge Report Directive 74
Baldridge, Colonel 71
Baltic Sea 123
Bari 42, 96, 103, 149, 152, 167
Barth, Germany 120, 125, 133
Basei, Pietro 33
Bates, Willie 181
Bayeux, France 21
Belgrade, Yugoslavia 45, 150
Belzig, Germany 132
Berlin, Germany 14
Bertelli, Alfred 22, 26
Best, Leon 206
Biason, Gino 28-29
Biason, Nevio 28
Biason, Rosino 27
BIG FENCE 162, 174
Birch, Ernest 88, 95
Birkenau 143
Bishop, Bob 160, 163-165, 167, 171, 174
Black March 125
Blechhammer, Germany 14
Blodgett, Dan 103-104, 110-112, 119-120, 123, 133, 135, 137-138, 143-144
Bobier, Bob 45-46, 48-50, 52-55, 57, 60, 67, 209
Boehme, Richard 160-163, 167-170, 174-175
Bolestaw, Rudek 114
Bologna 5
Bolzano 5

Bond, John 203, 205
Bos Novi 94
Bourassa, Lionel 78, 83
Bracciano, Lake 4
Brandon, George 81, 84-85
Breen, Jack 143
Bright, James 209, 212
Brittin, Eugene 22, 27, 29-30, 32, 34, 39-40, 127
Brown, Bob 160, 163
Brown, Ormiston 22
Broz, Josip 19
Bruck, Austria 178, 181-182, 189, 193, 196
Bucharest, Romania 210
Budapest, Hungary 149
Buel, Charles 212
Bulgaria 18
Bulge, Battle of 15
Bunney, Norman 130
Burling, Robert 147
Burney, Morris 203, 207
Buster, Ray 88-89, 94
Byzantine 15

C

Cairns, Douglas 12
Cairo, Egypt 66
Cambridge 12
Cameron, James 146-149, 157
Campolita, Pat 100, 124
Canin, Paul 104-105, 107, 109-111, 118-120, 123, 125, 129, 133-135, 138-141, 143-144

Capri, Italy, Isle of 13
Carlson, Arthur 206
Carter, Jack 119
Carthage 15
Casablanca Conference 3
Castellano, General 5
Castelluccio, Italy 14
Cathcart, Joe 203, 206
Cerignola, Italy 14
Chaplin, George 209, 212
Chesterton, George 46-47, 50, 67
Chetniks 18, 20, 97, 150-151, 169
Chicago Cubs 99
Childers, Max 88, 92, 94
Chiossi 43
Christensen, Vernon 100-101, 107, 109-113, 119, 121-123, 126, 128-134, 138, 140-144
Churchill, Winston 3
Churen, Bulgaria 210
Cincinatti Reds 99
Combs, Paul 207
Conegliano, Italy 32
Cordovado, Italy 27
Cotterman, Lynn 200
Crete 149
Croatia 172
Croats 19
Crouchley, John 210-211
Cullen, Joseph 157
Culver, Bill 159-163, 165-167, 169-172, 175
Czakoczi, Ed 147
Czechoslovakia 18

D

D'Amico, Ferdinando 43
D'Olivo, Caterina 31-32
D'Olivo, Maria 32
D'Olivo, Umberto 31-32
Daehn, Arthur 178, 183
Dalmatian coast 170
Dameron, Charles 46-50, 56, 67, 69, 73-74
Daneluzzi, Gianna 43
Danube River 47-48, 87, 209
Darlington, Lt. 65
Disharoon, Homer 100
Doyle, Dick 48, 50, 53-54, 57-60, 67, 69, 71, 73-74
Duecker, Charles 204
Duffield, Joseph 205

E

Eaker, Ira 68
Eddy, Nelson 136
Eggers, Marcella 136-137
Eggers, William 105
Eisenhower, Dwight D. 6
Emmanuel, Victor, (King) 4

F

Field, Charles 204
Fifty Missions from Broadway 87, 89, 93, 98
Flak Shak 127
Florence, Italy 15
Foggia, Italy 6-8

Frankfurt on Main 81, 119, 121
Frohnleiten, Austria 189
Fuerst, Laura 182, 196

G

Gable, Clark 12
Gansell, Stuart 9
Garner, Richard 100
General Butler 133
Geneva Convention 66, 71
Gestapo 18
Gillett, James 204
Giurgiu, Romania 47, 209
Glavan, Anka 166
Glavan, Marija 164-166, 175
Goldman, Abe 160, 162-163
Gordon, Mary 157
Grady, Gerald 209, 212
Gran Sasso Hotel 4
Graz, Austria 161, 190
Greece 18
Greenburg 31
Griefeldin, Germany 130
Griggs, Lawrence 22-23, 27, 29, 39, 41
Gross Tyschow 123
Grupchin, Bulgaria 58
Gultz, Germany 130
Gypsies 19

H

Hackler, Joe 146, 149, 152, 154
Halcomb, Dewey 206

Osterreichische Engine Works 92

Ouachita University 101

P

Padova, Italy 32

Palmer, Charles 46-47, 50-52, 56, 65, 67, 74

Paludo, Italy 30

Pancrazio, Italy 14

Pantanella, Italy 14

Panther 179-180

Parchim, Germany 130

Parise, Stephen 178

Partisans 18, 20, 49, 52, 96-97, 149, 169, 188

Patrick Henry, Camp 134

Patrk, Sime 169

Patton, George 35

Paul Hamilton S.S. 46

Pavelic, Ante 19

Perillo, Ralph 211

Peros, Nikica 168, 175

Peros, Niko 168

PFF 104

Phelts, Angus 25

Philippines 45, 87

Piave River 33

Pierce, Edgar 207

Pierced Steel Planking 8

Pittsburgh Pirates 99

Pizzolitto, Alugia 28

Ploesti, Romania 14, 47, 53, 159

Po River 4

Poland 18

Pope John Paul II 139

Pordenone, Italy 27

Portogruaro, Italy 29, 43

Pratt, Frank 102-103, 109-110, 113, 119-121, 129, 133-134, 138, 143

Presotto, Antonio 33

Privlaka, Yugoslavia 164

R

Rabinovitz, Morris 181

Rams, Antoni 116

Rasco, Art 87-89, 92-95, 97-98

Reagan, Bernard 181

Red Cross 11, 13, 34-35, 59, 120, 122-123, 127-128, 149, 191

Reddington, Malachi 209

Regensburg, Germany 170

Reims, France 195

Rice, Donald 137

Ridgeway, Mr and Mrs. 185

Ring, Henry 178, 184-185, 188, 195-196

Robbins, Jack 209, 212

Roberts, Jesse 79

Roehn, Donald 206

Romania 18, 45, 64

Rome, Italy 13, 21

Roosevelt, Franklin 3, 120

Rosenthal, Joe 177

Roth, David 204

Rucker, William 78, 79, 82

Ruse, Bulgaria 209

Russell, Joe 184, 196, 197
Russians 19
Ryan, Bill 178, 180, 182-183,
185-196

S

Salerno, Italy 6
Salonika, Greece 145-149, 157
San Giovanni, Italy 14
Sandall, John 75-77, 83
Saracens 15
Sawyer, Edward 205
Scheer, Friedrich 26, 43
Schwester Albana 80
Sellers, John 181, 188
Serbs 19
Sharpe, Jim 9
Sharpe, Laura 172
Sharpe, Lemar181
Shelor, Marion 203, 207
Sheridan, Murray 22-24, 42
Shields, Merl 179-180, 184-185,
188-189, 195, 197
Shriner, Major 80
Shumen, Bulgaria 61, 64-65, 67,
69, 209
Sicily 4
Sideratos, Christopher 46, 50,
52, 67
Siegenburg, Germany 203
Siegfried Line 45
Sikora, Sgt. 116, 128, 138
Silva, Lawrence 204
Sjodin, Daniel 39, 101

Skoblar, Marija 170-171, 175
Skopje, Yugoslavia 59, 61, 72,
74, 149
Skrzynska, Janina 117-118
Skrzynska, Maria 116-118, 144
Slackaway, Albert 79
Slovenians 19
Smith, Cecil 157
Smith, Claude 181
Smith, Walter 45, 47, 49-50,
53-55, 62-63, 65-69, 71-72, 74,
149, 209-210
Sniegowski, William 178, 185,
188-189, 196-197
Sofia, Bulgaria 49, 61, 65-66, 69,
71, 151-152
South, Joe 25-26, 43
Spinazzola, Italy 14, 76, 145
Sportman's Park 99
SS 18, 27, 32, 41, 129, 141
St. Avold 15
St. Louis Cardinals 99
St. Michele al Tagliamento, Italy
29
Stalag 9C 80, 85
Stalag Luft I 82, 120, 128, 131,
133
Stalag Luft III 34
Stalag Luft IV 123, 125, 128-129,
131, 141, 144
Stanev, Stanimir 73, 210
Stauverman, Ed 103
Stergulc, Fabio 41, 43
Stewart, Jimmy 12
Stewart, Joe 88, 95

Wels, Austria 177
Wetzlar, Germany 120
Whatley, Jack 178, 196
White, Hugh 204
White, Tom 146, 152-157
Whiting, Wayne 9
Whitney, J.H. 74
Whorton, William 203, 205
Wichmann, Art 100, 124
Wiggins, Volney 102
Wiktor, Stefan 115, 137, 144
Wilson, John 211
Winter, George 103-104,
    109-110, 113, 133-134, 138, 143
Wolf, Irvin 206

X Y Z

Yates, Robert 178, 185, 188, 195
Yellow G 77
YMCA 64
Yugoslavia 18-20
Zafirov, Peter 58, 71, 74
Zagreb, Yugoslavia 171
Zara, Yugoslavia 20, 162, 169,
    188
Zaton, Yugoslavia 169
Zemke, Colonel 83
Zoric, Jakov 167
Zygodowice, Poland 114, 137,
    139

The Author

Jerry Whiting is a South Dakota native and a graduate of the University of California, Santa Barbara, with a Bachelor of Arts degree. He later earned a Master's Degree at John F. Kennedy University.

Jerry worked in Law Enforcement for 28 years in the San Francisco Bay Area, holding a variety of positions. During his unique career he had an opportunity to work with police departments in several European countries, studying tactics and procedures and also spent a brief period as an observer with the Cheyenne River Tribal Police in South Dakota.

He has written two other books about World War II. His first book was *I'm Off to War, Mother, But I'll Be Back: Reflections of a WWII Tail Gunner.* This is a biography of his father's combat experiences on a B-24 bomber over Europe and the promise made to his family to return safely. His other book in print is *Veterans in the Mist: World War II Memoirs of the Third Thursday Lunch Bunch.* This is a book about a group of World War II Vets who live near him who meet monthly to share memories. It contains personal accounts of the experiences of more than 20 of these men, from the jungles of New Guinea to the Ardennes Forest, and beyond. He travelled extensively to research the stories for his books.

In addition, he has produced two documentaries. The first, *In the Shadow of Mt. Vulture: Venosa Then and Now* is a film about 15th Air Force airmen stationed in Italy and answers the question of whether their efforts and sacrifice are still remembered today in southern Italy. The second and most recent documentary, *New Year's at Ramitelli: A Safe Haven for Change*, is the heartwarming story the men of one bomb group in Italy and their unique relationship with the "Red Tails", the famed Tuskegee Airmen, told by two of the participants.

The author regularly assists other researchers here and abroad. He has consulted and provided training for the Dept. of Defense (DPMO) on MIA issues. He is currently the Historian for the 485th Bomb Group Association and served as publisher for their group history, *Missions by the Numbers: Combat Missions Flown by the 485th Bomb Group (H)*. Jerry has written numerous articles for periodicals and magazines and is often called upon as a guest speaker, where he always emphasizes the importance of preserving our rich American history and the lessons to be learned from it. He teaches part-time and he and his wife live in Walnut Creek, California.

You may contact the author directly for signed copies of his books or with questions or comments at: EAJWWhiting@aol.com.

You can read more about his books and documentaries at www.jwhitingwarstories.com.

Made in the USA
San Bernardino, CA
02 June 2016